Josh -

"The enemy of the) is arriving"

Never stop thriving

powerfully impact others!

Larry Joe

Other Resources From Jamey Schrier:

To access additional resources, visit

www.TheAutomatedProfessionalPractice.com

The Automated Practice

Success Secrets for Working Less and Earning More

DR. JAMEY T. SCHRIER

THE AUTOMATED PRACTICE: Success Secrets for Working Less and Earning More

by Dr. Jamey T. Schrier

Copyright © 2016 by Jamey Schrier.

Published by: Town Schrier Publishing

Inquiries should be addressed via email to support@jameyschrier.com, or visit: *www.TheAutomatedProfessionalPractice.com*

ISBN: 978-0-9976918-0-1 Paperback Edition
        978-0-9976918-1-8 Digital Edition

Library of Congress Control Number: 2016909974

Author services by Pedernales Publishing, LLC
www.pedernalespublishing.com

Printed in the United States of America

Dedication

This book is dedicated to my wife, Colleen, for her unwavering support allowing me to follow my passion. I love you. To Jack and Gracie, who inspire me every day to be the best father and role model. To Jesse Elder, my mentor and spiritual gangster. To Lee Brower and the entire Strategic Coach team for encouraging me to write and finish this book. A special thank you to Steve Thompson for writing the foreword and for demonstrating what it is to be a lighthouse. I want to send special appreciation to the Schrier PT team whose dedication and professionalism allowed me to explore my purpose. And finally, to all of the practice owners out there who are transforming and positively impacting the world...I appreciate you all.

Table of Contents

Foreword

Owning and running a physical therapy practice can be a lonely place. As a private practice owner, you can often feel as if you're on an island, with no way to navigate back home to a safe place, much less a prosperous place. This experience is especially true for physical therapy owners, as most have had little to no business training and rely on growing their practices based on what they do best—treating patients.

Most physical therapists who become practice owners choose this path in search of more freedom, whether it is the freedom of more time or more money… or both. This was certainly my goal when I purchased my first office from my former partner. As I expanded and opened a second clinic closer to home, I found myself trapped, working seven days a week. I searched for answers amongst my peers, but I found that most of my fellow owners were caught up in a negative mindset stemming from tough challenges they faced in the irrevocably broken healthcare system. This negativity really affected me during my early years as an owner… I even contemplated quitting my physical therapy business completely and changing careers.

Like most owners, I had started my practice wanting more time, more money, and more freedom to do it "my way." But I quickly realized that I had none of these things. In reality, I was working 60-70 hours per week, had very little money, and hated my professional life. My business results were dismal and I wanted a way out. I realized then that rather than me owning my PT practice, my PT practice really owned ME.

As such, I began a new quest to fix the problems in my practice that were causing excess stress in my life. I needed to change the many sleepless nights, the increased tension with my family, and the fact that I was rarely ever "present" during family vacations and other events. I needed to change the fact that I brought my computer everywhere and logged in on a daily basis, never relaxing and fully enjoying those moments with my wife and kids.

During my quest, I worked with industry consulting companies designed to teach me management "technology" and sure-fire fixes for the woes of my practice. However, after spending lots of money and lots of travel time with minimal and sometimes negative results, I realized that working with these companies was not the solution for me, and I decided to change directions.

Next, I began diving deep into business books. I learned some interesting and helpful information but found no quick fixes or comprehensive, permanent solutions. The books I read either weren't specific to private practices, or did not have real action-oriented strategies that I could immediately implement into my practice.

Then I met Jamey. When I did, he provided me with simple and highly-effective concepts and strategies to get my practice to work FOR me. Jamey presented workable solutions that helped me create my own "automated" private practice. A few of my favorite concepts from Jamey are the Time Management System, the Evergreen No Doc Lunch Marketing Program, the Simple Financial Dashboard, and all of the Mindset strategies. The concepts I learned from Jamey put me on the path to more time, more money, and more freedom. Jamey helped me realize that the destiny of my practice was in my hands, and he empowered me to make the practice improvements happen and change my life.

In the two years that I've known Jamey, he has helped me engineer a six-figure turnaround in profitability. Additionally, implementing Jamey's concepts has improved the workflow of my practice, allowing me greater flexibility in money, freedom, and time. This has resulted in office morale being at an all-time high and my productivity skyrocketing. But best of all, my family is much happier with me and I live my life with a positive attitude.

All of these successes that I have achieved are the result of the concepts and strategies that are now available to you in this book. I consider this book to be the bible on how to effectively and efficiently build and run a private practice. In this book, Jamey shares the experiences and insights that have come from his 15-year career as a business owner running a successful, multi-clinic physical therapy practice.

Because of Jamey and his method of teaching, I was able to put into place systems and processes that have empowered my staff, streamlined my hiring processes, and exploded our marketing. With a greater sense of clarity regarding the various areas of my practice, I quickly added $9,000 per month to my profit margin.

My life has been forever changed since meeting and working with Jamey. The concepts he shared with me two years ago are now available in this book. These concepts are the exact things that have helped fuel my practice's growth and my personal growth to levels that I thought were completely unattainable— especially in such a short time period. By continually applying these principles in my practice, I have created more time for my family, have gained greater income, and am the happiest I have ever been than at any point in my 15 years as a practice owner.

The Automated Practice contains incredible concepts, strategies, and tactics that will empower you to overcome the struggles so familiar to many owners. In this book, Jamey does not just repackage and regurgitate other people's principles; he has personally created his principles based on his experience in developing an extremely successful self-managed practice in Washington, D.C.

When you approach this book for the first time, do so with an open mind, a bigger vision, and a belief that life can be better. Success and abundance are the only outcomes possible when implementing Jamey's simple philosophy of building your business.

Personally, I have read numerous books on building a business, taken extensive coursework on improving a business, and listened to all of the "experts" out there. However, if I had been given this book first, I could have saved myself countless hours of pain and misery, used the many thousands of dollars spent on other consultants to explode my business to even greater levels, and avoided costly mistakes.

Now it is up to you. Sit down, fasten your seatbelt, and commit yourself to your success. I promise that it will happen to you, just as it did for me, by following the simple steps contained in *The Automated Practice.*

Steve Thompson, MPT
Owner of Sport and Spine Therapy of Marin

THE AUTOMATED PRACTICE

PART 1

THE INSPIRATION

"Daddy," tears welled up in his eyes as he looked at me, "I hate that you're never home." I sat silently, pondering what to say. How could I explain to him that I had to work all of those hours so we could afford our lifestyle? My son could barely count to ten.

Thankfully, this sad image was never repeated. But it was where my life was headed had I not created my *Automated Practice*. Yet, an increasing number of physical therapists are exchanging their families and personal lives for more hours in the clinic—a needless and avoidable sacrifice.

I am no stranger to money troubles. My parents were riddled with financial instability, which constantly held a black cloud over their relationship. This continuous shadow hung on every decision our family made and eventually clung to my siblings and me.

My parents taught me the lessons of frugality, but negative connotations of money also accompanied those lessons. I knew how to stretch a dollar, even if it meant bargaining more of my time and energy to save that dollar. This subconscious view of money affected how I opened my practice, hired staff, marketed, and handled my finances. A dark, anxious malaise persisted throughout my life, and this same worry began to take a toll on my own relationship with my wife. It seemed that I would be doomed to never offer enough to my family whether it be my time or wallet.

Because my mother judged wealthier people to be better than my family, I too always harbored a grudge. I would scrutinize those with money; I would pick apart their character and look for their faults. What I failed to realize is that this type of behavior only poisoned me.

I opened my PT practice in 2001, and like many physical therapists living the nightmare, I was also headed down a path to disaster. I had to work 60-80 hours per week. I was seeing over 70 patients a week. I simply had too much on my plate. And on top of all of that, I had a very negative attitude that was twisting and spoiling anything I accomplished.

> *I had finally reached my breaking point and my world was imploding.*

I had finally reached my breaking point and my world was imploding. The walls and artificial barriers I had erected grew unstable. I was nearing a complete breakdown. It was during that time that life threw me a curveball.

My practice burned down in 2004. This catastrophic event ironically brought me peace instead of despair. During this time of relative tranquility, life laid two choices in front of me: I could do what I knew, work over 60 hours a week with little money and time for my family or I could completely change my practice and working methodology.

I sided with the latter and went to work crafting the largest paradigm shift that would manifest within my life. Creating and implementing my Automated Practice Model literally saved my life. My model, which I will explain throughout the remainder of this book, has made the most profound change in my happiness, as well as generating greater monetary profits.

I began to open my eyes to a world where money was no longer the "root of all evil." If you remember studying back in high school and college, you will recall that money is a lot like vectors. Money is a force—a magnitude—and the hands it is exchanged through determine its direction. Humans drive the power of money for good or evil, and so it was my turn to earn my fair share to make some good of that power.

On top of that revelation, I began delegating and trusting in my colleagues. I realized that I hated operating the business side of my clinic. Not only that, but my plate was too full to manage these responsibilities properly. I would much prefer to delegate the work of marketing, accounting, dealing with insurances, and so on. My most enjoyable work was doing what I had trained so many years to do: help others by offering the best physical therapy possible.

One pleasant side-effect of delegation was that my employees and PTs always did a better job than I did. In addition to providing better service, my income grew while my stress levels decreased and more free time became available to me. In a matter of months, my income levels soared while my stress levels sank. I spent more time at home and began to truly live. It was no longer necessary for me to always be "on-site" at my clinic.

Because I invested in mentors and changed my whole approach to my business, I was finally able to achieve freedom. The freedom to be financially secure. The freedom to have time with family and take vacations. The freedom to choose the patients and doctors with whom I really want to work. The freedom to live the life I was born to live while serving people who could benefit from my gifts and unique destiny.

I'm Dr. Jamey Schrier and the purpose of this book is to share my journey to help you achieve professional freedom. Along the way, I will teach you strategies and techniques that enabled me to rebuild a struggling practice that was barely generating $350,000 per year while working six days a week, into an organized, smooth-operating, seven-figure PT business.

And, more importantly, I will show how YOU can use this knowledge to explode your own practice. Here is what we will be covering:

- I am going to share with you how my burnt-down office helped me build a $1.4 million practice, with over $250,000 in profit, while taking an astounding 137 days off work.
- More specifically, I'm going to show you how I discovered, through years of trial and error, the Automated Practice Model that I use today.
- I'm going to show you how to turn times of financial uncertainty, from low insurance reimbursements, increased competition, and government interference, into enormous opportunity and growth for you.
- I will take you inside the Automated Practice Model and show you exactly how to turn your current practice into an organized, smooth operating, profitable business.

CHAPTER 1

Referrals on Demand

Referrals are the lifeblood of my practice. I'm going to show you how to get referrals on demand and how to increase the number of referrals that are coming into your practice from doctors and doctors' practices. But before I do that, I want to briefly outline for you how all of this came to be in 2004, just after my practice burned down.

Prior to the fire, I felt stressed. I constantly had this uneasy feeling and experienced recurring waves of anxiety. The reason was evident to me: I was upset that I didn't have the balance I was looking for, the balance of family time versus business.

Unfortunately, my life balance was about 80 percent business and only 20 percent family. I knew that this was *exactly* what I didn't want. So, how was I going to changeover this balance between work and home? At the time, I was seeing 60 or 70 patients a week—not bad for being the only physical therapist in the practice. Although I was anxious, stressed, and confused about how I was going to change my situation, I felt good about being busy. Well, until the fire happened.

Once I made the decision to change my life balance, I came back into the practice with an entirely new attitude. I wanted to build and grow my practice and create a business where I could have more freedom to take time off and more money to better provide for my family. I knew I had to start doing things differently. I also knew that consistent marketing would be the key.

Prior to the fire, I only had two doctors referring one to two patients a month to me. Most of my business was word-of-mouth because my patients really enjoyed my treating methodology.

When I got back into the office I was ready for things to change. I thought the fastest way to boost my referrals was to engage with the local doctors. Like most owners before me, I started with lunches. I went to the doctors' offices and said, "Hey, I'd like to set up a meeting to introduce myself to the doctor." The administrative person would reply, "Sure. Can you bring in lunch?" I thought to myself, "Have lunch with the doctor? This is better than I thought."

Much to my surprise, the conversation with the office coordinator went something like this: "We have 20 people on staff, so you need to bring enough for 20. We've got a few vegetarians, and we really like this lunch place that delivers delicious sandwiches…" I timidly replied, "Okay," not realizing this lunch was going to set me back between $400 and $500.

I thought this was the way to do it and at least I would get to meet the doctor and build a relationship that would get me tons of referrals.

Unfortunately, here's what typically happened. I went to the office and they immediately took me back to the lunch room. I took pride in setting up a beautiful spread including a centerpiece. The staff loved it. Many of them introduced themselves and thanked me for lunch.

I anxiously waited in the lunchroom for the doctor to show. Finally, the doctor came in about 30 minutes late and said, "Hey, how are you doing?" He didn't really know who I was or even the fact that I was a PT.

The doctor sat down for a few minutes for some small talk. He asked me who I was and a couple of other general questions.

About five minutes later he ended the meeting with, "Jamey, I really appreciate the lunch. We'll send you tons of patients." Sometimes, he would even add in how good we were. Then he left.

To be perfectly honest, I felt really good about myself after the first few doctor lunches. I thought, "Holy smokes. I just brought in some lunch and this doctor is going to send tons of patients to me. I could do this all day long."

I did this type of marketing for months. Every week I would bring in lunch for doctors racking up thousands of dollars in marketing costs. Many times I would get a patient or even two from a doctor, but it never lasted.

I started to question whether this was the best method to generate referrals. Initially, the numbers looked good. Let's say a new patient was worth $1,000 if they came in for the entire plan of care. If I did $1,000 to $2,000 for every doctor lunch and my profit margin was 20 percent, then I was making $400 to $800. Not bad, right?

Then I started looking at how much it was costing me—$400 to $500 for lunch, plus two hours of travel and set-up time. I began thinking this is only going to work if they send me consistent patients without me having to continually sponsor lunches.

That never happened. There would be an initial spike of new patients. Then it would gradually return to zero unless I brought lunch again. So I did. I reasoned, "If that's what it takes to generate referrals, then that's what it takes." So I brought lunches to each doctor's office every three months.

Not only did I feel like a cheap prostitute doing this, I realized that this was NOT the way to build my practice. I wasn't building any meaningful relationships with physicians who appreciated what I did. There was no long-lasting value-building. Basically, I was buying a couple of referrals for the price of a lunch.

I thought to myself, "You know what? This is not for me." I went back to the marketing drawing board and said, "All right, if I was a doctor, what would I think about physical therapy?" I wasn't really sure. I didn't have the answer to that question.

I decided to get the answer from the proverbial horse's mouth. I spoke to a couple of doctors that I knew. They were friends of mine so I knew they would be honest.

"What do you think about physical therapy?" I asked.

They replied, "We love it."

So I continued, "Well, when do you refer a patient to physical therapy or how do you decide to refer?" Each of them told me when and how they referred and most importantly, who they refer to.

I got the bright idea to start asking other doctors these same questions, many of whom referred patients to me. It was basic market research. And the feedback was eye-opening.

I discovered that the majority of doctors I spoke to didn't refer patients to me because I was the best PT. They didn't refer because I was the best manual therapist. They didn't refer because of my passion and caring nature or because I took care of people better than anyone. None of those were the real reason why they referred to PT.

Instead, these doctors referred based on three things:

1. Location
2. Insurances you accept
3. Specificity

Wow. That was a bit of an ego check.

Contrary to what I thought, referrals had very little to do with my skills, performance, or reputation. Even specificity—whether or not the PT had a specific niche, was low on the reasons for referrals.

Although I didn't like the answers they gave me, nor did I agree with them, I wanted to increase referrals quickly.

I thought, if they view physical therapy as nothing more than a commodity (i.e., physical therapy is physical therapy; one PT is not much different from another), then how could I use this knowledge to build referrals? As a physical therapist who has invested a small fortune in my post-graduate education, I knew that there was a huge difference between PTs. Unfortunately, that wasn't a huge interest to them.

Looking at it from their perspective, what were my choices? It only came down to two: I could either change their minds or I could initially play along until I got consistent referrals.

My strategy was to educate those referred patients, show them the value of my services and what I do, and then I could hopefully turn those patients into a referral machine for my practice (we'll discuss this more in later chapters). I looked at it as a two-step process. The bottom line was that if I didn't have the patient in my practice in the first place, I would have nothing more than empty slots.

So, I could either stand on my soapbox and tell all of those doctors what I thought they should be thinking about PT, or I could accept the fact that they have a particular view about PT and engage with them at their level. I chose to engage with them at their level.

First, I stopped throwing away time and money on lunches for doctors. If doctors like referring to physical therapy, then the real question I should be asking is how do they refer to physical therapy?

In other words, how does the patient get from the doctor's office to my PT practice? Basically, I just needed to know *how each doctor and each doctor's office liked to refer patients out to physical therapy*. I changed my strategy from bringing in lunches to instead, engaging with their front desk person. In my experience, this seemed like the person most likely to know how the office handled referring to PT.

Here's the script I used:

"Hello, my name is Jamey and I'm from Schrier Physical Therapy. What's your name?" That was it. That was my opening line.

"*Hi, my name is Tiffany.*"

"Hi, Tiffany. How are you doing today? I see that you're pretty busy. Is it one of those crazy days?"

"*Every day is crazy. What can I do for you?*"

"I just have a couple of quick questions. Do you have a minute?" The key is to actually listen to see what Tiffany's answer is.

Sometimes Tiffany would say, "*I'm really busy right now.*"

If so, then I would say something to the effect, "Great. I can call back later. What's a good time?"

I wasn't going to push my agenda at the expense of bulldozing Tiffany. I wanted to first and foremost respect her time. My initial goal was to build rapport with Tiffany and then ask her a couple of questions. Her answers would help me decide my next step.

I did not go in there with this line, "Hey, how you doing? My name is Jamey. I'm from Schrier Physical Therapy—we're located down the street. We're really good at PT. We do manual physical therapy and really care about our patients. We do phenomenal work. We do sports and orthopedics. Here are some cards and prescription pads."

THAT DOESN'T WORK.

You're throwing information at them because you're nervous and want to get the heck out of there as quickly as possible. I understand. I used to be that person.

However, this time, I was there to convey a feeling. I was there to engage and be interested in her. Since she said she was busy, I didn't want to ignore that fact. Instead, I went with it. If the front desk person was busy, I'd make arrangements to come back at a better time.

If she had a few minutes, we'd talk. But that doesn't happen until that initial rapport is built. Sometimes, it may take more than a couple of minutes to build rapport. You may have to come back if they're busy. That's just the reality of it, so you have to be sensitive to the situation. The best way to develop that sensitivity is to visit a lot of offices.

I'd start with a couple of general questions and those would lead into the more specific questions.

"Listen, I can't imagine how busy you must be. How long have you been here?"

"I've been here for six months."

"Great, do you like it?"

"Yeah, I do like it, but it gets crazy sometimes."

"I hear you. My staff says the same thing sometimes. Can I ask you a question? Do you ever use physical therapy for your patients?"

"Of course. All of the time."

"Oh, that's cool. What kind of patients do you refer?"

"Oh, we refer patients with back pain."

"That's great. What has been your experience referring to various physical therapists?"

Now I'm getting her experience behind it. I would just continue to ask her a few more questions until my biggest question:

"How does the patient actually get to the physical therapy place? How do you choose where they go?"

Now because I already had a little bit of knowledge of doctors' tendencies, sometimes I would load the question with, "Is it based on location or insurance primarily?"

Now it's time to let her tell you the referral pattern.

"No. If a doctor wants the patient to have PT, they usually give

the patient a script then the patient comes to me and asks me where to go."

Bingo. Now I know who the most important person in that doctor's office is… and it's NOT the doctor. It's the front desk person.

If this was the case, every strategy I could think of would be to better engage and create a relationship with the front desk person. I would go into the office with reports, candy, and especially something personal that I know they would like. The more specific it was to the individual, the better.

What was the result? My numbers started to grow and it didn't cost me a thing (except time, of course). Once I became too busy in the clinic or tired of visiting offices, I hired someone who could naturally build relationships with people. My numbers increased even more because my marketing representative did a better job than I did.

I discovered that many offices have *lists*. Lists consist of PT practices and other ancillary services that doctors, especially orthopedists, often refer to.

Why do they have lists? Because like us, doctors are getting reimbursed less and less money and have a limited amount of time.

Providing a list of PT practices and allowing the patient to choose where to go based on location and insurances they accepted saved the doctor hours of time. As a PT, I wasn't happy with this, but I decided to make the best out of this situation.

My new patient numbers shot up after discovering this little tidbit. I just asked the front desk person, once rapport was established, if our name could be added to their referral list. I had my marketing person go to every orthopedic group in the area that used lists and asked to have our clinic added to those lists.

Now remember, the referral source may not be the front desk person; it might be the office manager. It's whoever can answer the questions. Sometimes you might start off with the front desk person, the receptionist or whomever, and then you could say, "How do you refer?"

"Oh, well, the office manager, Marie, takes care of that."

"Great. Is it possible to speak with Marie?"

"She's busy right now but I can set up a time for you to come and speak to her."

"That would be great. I just want to talk to her and really understand a little bit more about how you do things."

"Yeah, sure."

If you have rapport with the front desk, getting a meeting with Marie and building a relationship gets a little easier. The bottom line is that you want to speak with the person who knows the answer to the single biggest question:

How do they refer out to physical therapy?

My experience, having used this strategy over the last 10 years, is most family practices and internal medicine offices are much more concerned with what insurances you accept, but don't have a list. Their mindset is like that because *they* accept everything in the world and only want the best for their patients, which means the cheapest.

Surgeons, orthopedists, and neurologists are not as concerned with the insurances. Obviously, the landscape is changing, so doctors' habits will adapt and referral patterns will change.

Since I was out-of-network with most insurances, I found it uncomfortable when they asked me, "Are you in network?"

I learned very quickly that offices that weren't so focused on insurances were better referral sources for me.

Once I got busy, which didn't really take that long at all (only a few weeks going to a number of offices), I felt that I really enjoyed the treating aspect of my business more than networking and marketing. I made a decision to hire someone who could help me do that. I scripted out for her exactly what I shared with you above. Her job was to go to doctors' offices and build rapport.

She would ask the front desk person the same questions: Does the office refer to physical therapy? If so, how do they do that?

Many times when I was doing my front office visits (that's what we called them), they would actually ask me if I wanted to meet the doctor. Once rapport and genuine interest were established, I felt that many of them allowed me into their world behind the waiting room.

Now that I have given some of these anecdotal insights, let's move forward. Once I got the critical information of how the office referred to PT, two things happened:

1. My practice started to get tons of referrals—some from the relationship with the front desk or office manager, and others by just having my name on their list;
2. I began to use this strategy on over 400 doctors in the area.

Remember, prior to this strategy I only had two doctors referring a couple of patients per month.

At the time of writing this, we have over 300 doctors referring well over 100 new patients a month to us. Not bad for only having two small practices.

I went from being on nobody's PT list to being on everyone's list in the area. Offices began to know who I was (well, at least the front desk and the office managers did).

Now when patients ask the front desk person which PT they should see, most of the time they say, "Go to Schrier. They're really good."

My number one marketing strategy became staying focused on building rapport with the referring staff member and that sometimes led to a doctor meeting. Regardless, momentum and energy ramped up and our referrals reflected that.

Best of all, the entire marketing process was being done

completely by my marketing director, not me, once I had the system worked out. (We'll talk more about how to delegate in Chapter 6.)

My job transitioned to being more of a coach, helping troubleshoot any issues my marketing director was having. Since I had the experience of visiting offices myself, I could relate to whatever challenges she was having and help her solve them.

Many times, troubleshooting meant bringing in a little thank you gift to show our appreciation. The note would say something like, "Whether you referred anybody to us, or not, I just want to say thank you."

Appreciating the front desk goes a long way. My marketing director quickly realized that front desk people, especially in busy doctor's offices, go under-appreciated. She made it a point to show her appreciation every chance she got.

The result: my marketing director was able to triple the results I got while creating deeper and more meaningful relationships with those folks in the offices.

It may not have been the magic bullet that I was looking for, but it was the most powerful thing I learned in working with different doctors and their offices.

We have relationships with over 300 doctors today, and I can honestly say that I haven't met 90 percent of them. Yet, the practices remain busy and the patients remain happy, while the doctors' time remains respected.

As far as meeting doctors, these days I carefully choose which doctors I want to meet. I meet the ones who have mutual respect toward me and what I can offer.

That's the marketing strategy I use successfully and that I've shared with many, many other private practice owners. The good news: it has worked for every single one of them. And I know it can work for you.

DO NOT visit one office and then go back to your practice

and sit there and wait for the phone to ring. It doesn't work like that.

I recommend visiting 10-30 offices and building momentum while learning from your (or whoever is doing the visits) experiences. The confidence, knowledge, and experience you will gain from going to these offices will be incredible.

Before visiting doctors' offices, take a few minutes to form a strategy. Why are you going to see them? What will be your reason? What can you drop off?

To be clear, you're going into these doctors' offices to understand their view on physical therapy. Do they refer out? How do they do that? If it's a list, what do you have to do to get on the list? What's the criteria? What has to be done?

Build rapport the whole way through and keep doing this on a consistent basis.

That's it. That's all you have to do right now.

If you choose to delegate this, and I am a huge fan of delegating tasks, then do it.

If you feel your time is better spent managing the office, treating patients, or doing something else, that's okay. However, I would encourage you to go out to at least half a dozen offices and experience the process yourself so that you can be a resource for your marketing person.

Tip: Many doctors like National Provider Identifier (NPI) numbers. It just makes it easier to refer to you.

Questions to ask:

1. Do they refer out to PT?
2. Do they have a list?
3. How do they refer out?
4. How does a doctor choose one therapy practice over another?

Now, of course, when the patients come in, you're always looking for ways to connect back. So if a doctor refers somebody to you, obviously, you want to send them a follow-up report. Send a thank you letter, send a thank you email. I have found email is easy. A typewritten letter is a little more time consuming, but good. A handwritten note is the most powerful. It's up to you. You get to choose. This is common courtesy, thanking them for referring somebody to you. It's Acknowledgement 101, yet surprisingly few PTs take the time to send a thank you. It's one of those small touches that will make you stand out.

I've shared this system of generating referrals on demand and how to start getting new patients right away. I think it's simple. I think it's easy to understand and easy to do. I don't think it's complicated. I think what you will learn and the opportunities you'll gain will be phenomenal and it's something that I know will help you grow your practice.

For more information specifically on Chapter 1, Referrals on Demand, please visit:

www.TheAutomatedProfessionalPractice.com/book/chapter1

CHAPTER 2

The Unfair Advantage

Most people in the business world who are truly successful use the principles I will be covering in this chapter. First, let me begin by clarifying what I mean when I say "truly successful."

True success doesn't just refer to someone who makes a lot of money. There are numerous people in the world today who make a lot of money. Yes, most people would say that money is a part of success, but it isn't the only part. When I refer to successful people, I'm talking about having it all—not only having money, but making it in a way that is completely aligned with your natural gift or talent (what the great entrepreneurial coach Dan Sullivan calls "unique ability") and who you are.

I believe that to be truly successful, entrepreneurs must strive to create their lives and businesses around their unique abilities or, as some in the performance arena call it, "flow state." This chapter is not about diving into "flow state" or "unique ability." But I believe to be truly successful as a practice owner, you must create your business around your unique attributes. This will allow you to build a successful practice while staying authentic to yourself and what you love to do.

This chapter is on creating a successful practice using the principle that all of us have a natural expertise and passion, and by building your business around this passion, you will create incredible success and happiness.

Truly successful owners have a tremendous *imbalance* between work and home. Not the imbalance where an owner works 60 hours at the office and spends a few hours a week with the family. I'm referring to the type of imbalance where it's 80/20, home life to work life. When your practice is operating with vision, using efficiency and systems as your foundation, you can build this type of practice and have this type of life balance.

This wasn't always the case with me. As I mentioned before, I was operating my practice with stress and anxiety living inside me daily. Every decision was made out of reaction, not pro-action. I took very little time off and had very little time to myself.

"Truly successful" people have it all: Money, Time, Family, and most of all, Freedom to choose how you live your life. There's no better feeling than having the freedom to choose to go on a three-week family vacation and have the practice run significantly better than it did when you were there.

What I'm going to share with you in this chapter is something that, unfortunately, very few people know about and even fewer put into regular practice. However, those few people who do put it into practice are the truly successful people. The best part is that anyone can learn this and anyone can do it. Like anything else, it becomes a choice. Luckily, it was a choice that I made and one that hopefully you will make as well.

It's a choice that has allowed me to change my life and my children's lives. It has enabled me to transform a physical therapy practice of confusion and desperation into a self-managed, automated practice that allows me to be at the helm to do the things I'm really good at. It allows the people that I've hired to do the things they're good at.

This has allowed me to create a beautiful life with phenomenal people and a profitable business.

The First Step: Active Appreciation

The first step in creating the unfair advantage is called *Active Appreciation*. What exactly is Active Appreciation? It's a state of being fully and genuinely appreciative to someone or something.

Active Appreciation is different from being socially appreciative. Here is an example of social appreciation: "Jamey, would you like this cookie?" You say, "Yes. Thank you." Saying thank you shows appreciation, but in a socially, almost automatically accepted way. Saying please and thank you is polite and is something I believe we all, including myself, don't say enough. However, these types of social appreciations are more reactive in nature than proactive. In other words, someone has to do something for us in order for us to appreciate them or their action. What I'm talking about goes beyond that.

Active Appreciation is about appreciating someone or something whether they do anything for you or not. Let me give you an example. Here is one exercise that I do before I see a new patient.

> *Tip: Prior to going into the room to do my initial evaluation, I would ask myself this one question: "What do I appreciate about this person?"*

That question would immediately get me thinking about the patient, not myself. It helped me get into the right frame of mind. I wasn't going into the treatment room thinking that I was doing this person a favor. In fact, they were doing me a favor by trusting me with their time, money, and body. This one question completely changed the manner in which I treated anyone. Prior to that, I thought the patient was lucky to be seeing me. Let's face it, I was the best. Me, Me, Me. It was ALL about me.

This simple question completely revolutionized my thinking. I now say to myself, "I appreciate this person for taking action about their injury. Most people complain about their problems, but this patient is doing something about it. They're choosing a natural recovery method versus popping a bunch of pills." I also appreciated that they sought out physical therapy rather than the multitude of other choices. And lastly, that they chose Schrier Physical Therapy to help them.

This quick 30-second exercise done prior to seeing every patient (not just new patients!) completely transformed my mindset from a selfish one to a mindset of gratitude and appreciation.

And what happened in the evaluation? Something extremely powerful. The way I handled that evaluation, the way I listened to the patient, and the way I genuinely engaged with them was completely different from any other time prior to doing the Active Appreciation exercise.

As I implemented this custom, I realized more and more that I actually felt confident and positive going into these new patient evaluations. I didn't feel rushed or disheveled or unfocused. I felt extremely in the moment and centered.

> *Homework Assignment: Before your next evaluation or your next visit ask, "What do I appreciate about this person?" Quickly say what you appreciate to yourself. No one has to hear.*

It could be that they're trying to help themselves. You might take a quick look at their intake form and realize that they are a cancer survivor or have depression. Say something like this, *"You know, I really appreciate that this person is coming in for PT to see me, knowing that they're dealing with a lot of other stuff."* This person might say they're recently divorced. *"I really appreciate after all the crazy stuff that's happening in their life right now that they've taken the responsibility to come and help themselves."*

I promise this will put you in a better, more positive, and appreciative mental state.

To all of the cynics out there who are saying, "Thanks Jamey for the psychology lesson, but how is this supposed to help me build my practice?" I recommend just trying it.

I won't spoil it for you. I'll let you see for yourself what the results are. I will tell you this: there will be phenomenal things that stem from doing this exercise on a regular basis. The only way to know what they are is to put it to the test.

Active Appreciation has not only helped me with treating patients, but has also helped in other areas of my practice as well. For instance, I have been able to build a really great team of people at Schrier PT. However, this was not always the case. For years, I thought I had a revolving door in my practice, with staff coming and going seemingly every week. There was no consistency, culture, or sense of togetherness.

So, when I started rebuilding my team at Schrier, I asked that same question, "What do I appreciate about them?" I thought about each person on my team as an individual. "What do I appreciate about my front desk person?" I didn't ask just in terms of what she did for me, but I gave some thought as to who she was as a person and how she made each patient feel comfortable and welcome. I did this with all of my staff members.

In addition, I added this question to my staff meetings. I asked each person what they appreciated about another staff member. I, of course, went first and told each and every team member what I most appreciated about them.

As an example, for my front desk person Claudia, I said,

"Claudia, you are really great with people. You have a great heart and are very dependable. Plus, I can tell people really like you."

This approach changed my entire relationship with Claudia and everyone else on my team. Energy and productivity immediately shot through the roof. The togetherness that formed among the staff was incredible.

Prior to that, my meetings would consist of all of the negative things Claudia was doing at the front desk. All she heard was negative comments, especially from me, and worse, they were said publicly, not privately.

Most owners I have spoken with seem to have a contentious relationship with their staff, a Me versus Them mentality. In my experience, nothing breaks through that more than Active Appreciation.

> *Words hurt, but facial expressions, body language, and rolling of the eyes can hurt worse, especially over time.*

For those owners who don't actually say what they're feeling out loud, believe me, even if you don't say those negative thoughts to your staff, they can feel the negative vibe you're delivering to them; they can feel the negative energy and your disapproval. Words hurt, but facial expressions, body language, and rolling of the eyes can hurt worse, especially over time.

I start every meeting with an employee or manager, and every phone conversation or meeting with a referral source, with the most important question in the world: "What do I appreciate about them?" And the results of that have been astronomical. Although I studied all of the strategies on how to build a team, read the team-building books and went to all of the seminars, there was always something missing. There was something the books didn't teach me. I realized that the one component that was missing was something inside me, not in a book. It was the genuine appreciation of others and that has made all of the difference.

Celebrations and Wins

When I was growing up, there was a popular song that was played at every party, bar mitzvah, and wedding: *Celebration* by Kool and the Gang. It's a fun, upbeat song that is all about celebrating your achievements. I didn't realize that 25 years later, it would be one of the biggest game changers in my practice.

At Schrier PT, we take celebrations seriously. To me, a celebration is a form of appreciation and acknowledgment. Unfortunately, many of us do not acknowledge all of the little "wins" we've had as we've built our practices.

When I graduated physical therapy school from the University of Maryland, my parents took me out for a celebratory lunch with relatives and friends. This is quite normal for most of us. But, when was the last time you celebrated having the most visits in a week? How about the highest number of new patients in a month? How many of us even know when we have broken a record?

The point is that if we don't stop and acknowledge all of the wins we have achieved, then work becomes a negative, never-good-enough experience. I bet that anyone reading this book has told a person on their staff how well they did on something. But, how often have you told YOURSELF the same thing?

I used to be so hard on myself. Everything I accomplished was never good enough. I thought I could always do better. I could have seen one more patient. I bet we could have signed up one more new patient from an event.

This type of "never-good-enough" mindset almost destroyed my practice and my life. This same mindset also created that "revolving door" in my practice because the people around me never felt fully appreciated.

Here's an exercise that I do every day. I write down or acknowledge verbally one win I had from the previous day. What's a win? A win can be an achievement or even an experience as long as a lesson was learned.

Let's say you had a meeting with a doctor yesterday. Obviously that would be a win. It could be finally figuring out a solution for a difficult problem a patient was having. Wins can be big or small. It doesn't matter. What matters the most is that you are taking a few seconds to acknowledge them and that you are doing this daily.

What was your win yesterday?

Tracking wins for me was big, but using the win concept with my team was the real difference-maker. A couple of years ago I started to make this a regular thing during staff meetings. At the beginning of every staff meeting, we started off with a celebration or win. "What has been your biggest win in the last week?" I purposely wasn't specific. It could be professional, personal, patient-related, or not. It was their win. My job was to acknowledge it.

The power of the "celebration of wins" is in the acknowledgment and appreciation of the fact that you or your staff person did have a win, that something positive happened. It gives you (and them) an opportunity to say, "Good job, you did something well."

If you choose to add this to your staff meetings, my advice is to be patient with your staff. They may not fully trust you or realize why you're doing this. Allow them to say what their win is for the week or what they are most proud of.

The biggest lesson I have learned came from what happened after people shared their win with the group. Initially, I would comment on their win and dive in deeper as to why they said what they said. As a result, the staff shared less and less. My recommendation is to avoid questioning or commenting on their win. Just respond by saying, "Thank you, I appreciate you sharing that." That's it.

Be appreciative of the fact that they shared something with you and their colleagues. A beneficial thing that has happened is that I've learned more about my staff, what they like, what they do, and what's important to them than I've ever known about them before doing this exercise.

Something else will happen. Positivity. Most meetings that I held had a negative feeling to them. That was probably because I was stressed and very negative about many things: insurance companies, reimbursement, government, referral sources, and competition. This mindset naturally spilled over into my meetings.

I wasn't the only one. Your staff is also watching news and all of the disasters, bombings, killings, etc. Fear equals ratings, right? Adding positivity into their lives, if only their work lives, will have a dramatic effect on their outlook, interactions, and communications.

I have gone over Active Appreciation and celebrations and wins with respect to us, our patients, and our staff. How do you use it outside of the clinic when building relationships with referral sources?

Doctors

Let's say you're about to go into a doctor's office for a meeting. You're nervous and most likely you're going to talk non-stop and provide all kinds of information about how great you are as a PT, how much you care about your patients, how great your practice is, and so on. Try this instead. Before you walk in to meet with the doctor (or other referral source) ask yourself this question, "What do I appreciate about doctor so-and-so?" When I started doing this, my anxiety decreased as my appreciation factor increased. I felt more connected, less nervous, and have been able to create some amazing relationships that turned into referrals.

Here's just one of the things I appreciated about the doctors I've visited: they have invested hundreds of thousands of dollars in their education and have sacrificed personally throughout their early years, studying and learning their craft to help people live healthier lives.

Have you ever thought of a doctor like that before? When I walk into their office with that mindset, thinking, "This person has sacrificed a lot to get where they are and I totally appreciate that about them," there's no room for worry or fear, only appreciation.

Do you think I'm really nervous? No. Do you think I'm worried about all the questions they're going to ask me? No. It completely changed my whole demeanor with them. Now, I have conducted hundreds and hundreds of referral source meetings and for the first hundred or two, I was very nervous. But why? As I reflected back I realized why: because the meeting was all about me. I was nervous because I was worried that they were going to ask me questions I wouldn't know the answers to or they were going to challenge me on something. I was nervous because I wanted to make sure I could spew out all this great information about physical therapy and what I do and how I'm the best, etc.

When I walk into a meeting now I just start off the meeting by saying, "Doctor, I really appreciate you taking the time to meet with me today. I know you didn't have to do that. I know you have a very busy schedule. I know you work with a lot of people, and I just don't want that to go unsaid. I sincerely want to thank you for meeting with me."

How do you think that meeting goes after that? It goes a lot better than if I said, "Hi, Dr. Smith, my name is Jamey Schrier. I'm from Schrier Physical Therapy and thanks so much for meeting with me. I just want to tell you we do physical therapy and we're really the best, and here's some information, blah, blah, blah."

Of course, doctors love it when you do all of the talking because then they don't have to say a word. You leave not knowing anything more about the doctor. You've defeated the true purpose of the visit—to create a relationship with the doctor.

Active Appreciation reminds me that I am meeting a person, not just a referral source. We have a very relaxing, open conversation and make a *human* connection. The referrals we received started to increase without even having to ask for them.

Using the appreciation mindset with doctors resulted in a 300% increase in referrals. Our new patients went from 30-35 to well over 100 new patients per month. In addition, my relationships with the doctors were so much stronger.

I challenge you to try it the next time you visit a doctor or any referral source. Feel what happens when you enter their office compared to the times before.

I also use Active Appreciation when giving talks. I used to be extremely nervous when giving talks to groups, whether it was 10 people, 50 people, or 100 people. I decided to use the Active Appreciation mindset. Prior to the talk, I wrote down what I appreciated about my audience. For some reason, making that list calmed me down; my nervousness subsided considerably. I was still a little nervous, but when I spoke I became so much more connected with the audience. Of course, I started the talk with acknowledging that I really appreciated them being there that day.

Now let's summarize this whole Active Appreciation principle—the unfair advantage, as I like to call it. *What do I appreciate about...* (fill in the blank)? It can be your team at work, your patients, your referral sources, your audience, people coming up to your booth, or people at your events. What do you genuinely appreciate about them?

For those skeptics out there (and yes, I used to be one of you), this is basically a mind game. It's a psychological game you are having with yourself and the power of it is undeniable. If you practice Active Appreciation and you are genuine, you too will have phenomenal results. I have shared with you only a few of the areas in which I have used Active Appreciation. There are many other ways you can incorporate this concept into your business and your life.

The Second Step:
Avoiding the Negative Zone

The second and equally important step to creating an unfair advantage for you and your practice is recognizing and understanding something I call the "Negative Zone." The Negative Zone is a place that I used to spend A LOT of time in. In fact, I spent more time inside the Negative Zone than outside. Now, I can honestly say that although I still visit the Negative Zone from time to time, I'm very aware of when I'm in it and I have tools and tricks to get out quickly.

The Negative Zone is not simply a place of negativity, but a place of creative destruction, low energy, reactions, comparisons, judgments, and complaining.

To understand the Negative Zone is to understand our perspective on how we see things. Let me ask you a question: Do you believe there is such a thing as a horizon? You know, the edge of the Earth where the sun begins to show itself over yonder?

Of course there is (it wasn't a trick question). What if I asked you if you could ever get to the horizon? In other words, if you and I started walking towards the horizon today, would we get there? No way. Just like a rainbow, the horizon requires distance between you and it. It's something we can see, but never reach or touch.

I apply this horizon example to goal setting. Everyone knows that they should have a vision for their practice, an image of how they want things to operate. It may include a money vision, the number of days you want to have away from the practice, how many locations you want, or whatever else you can imagine. If you don't yet have a vision for your practice, then it definitely needs to become a high priority on your list because without a vision, it's hard to know where you're going. So the first thing for you to do is to create that vision and fix it in your mind.

You now have this vision of how things are going to be. However, the chances of this vision occurring exactly as you expect it to are slim to none. One of the reasons for this is as you get closer to your vision and realize it's more of a reality than a pipe dream, you'll begin to expand what you previously thought was possible.

Here's an example of what I mean.

If you're a physical therapy practice owner, at some point in your past you had a vision or dream of opening up a practice one day. Now that you have done that, I guarantee that your vision has expanded to either having multiple locations, multiple therapists, a certain number of new patients per month, or the number of days you want to be at the office. The closer you got to your vision, the further away it became because you naturally expanded it.

It's the same as the horizon example. The closer you get to the horizon the farther away it becomes. It's a constantly moving target.

Now let's say that instead of the word "vision" we use the word "ideal." The question you would ask yourself is, "What is my ideal practice?" You could even add a time frame to the question. "What will my ideal practice look like in two years?"

I'm going to show where we, as intelligent, full-of-drive PTs, go tragically wrong when moving toward our ideals, vision, or goals. Most of us (PT Owners) measure our progress forward toward the ideal we want. So, why is measuring your progress forward a bad thing?

If you measure your current progress forward against an ideal that's not only a future vision in your mind, but an expanding vision, you will ALWAYS feel like you fell short. Like you have failed.

Here's an example: I bet you have had tons and tons of successes and progress since starting your practice. I even bet you may have exceeded what you thought you were going to do.

Do you feel like it's still not good enough? Do you think that there's no time to feel good about your progress because of the challenges that continue to face you?

This is exactly how I felt for years. Like whatever I accomplished was never good enough. When people gave me kudos for things like starting a practice, hiring multiple staff, opening up a second location, cutting down my hours in the clinic, or even more recently, completely removing myself from the treatment schedule while continuing to increase business, all of those kind words and congratulations didn't mean much to me because I was still looking ahead. I was looking at an ideal that didn't exist except in my head. I never felt good about what I had accomplished for fear that I would become stagnant or lazy.

FINALLY I WOKE UP.

This "old" way of thinking measured all of my progress against this ideal or vision I had for my practice and my life. Here's how I view and measure my progress today:

Backwards.

Although I still use ideals and visions for direction so I know where I'm going, I measure my progress backwards against previous targets and accomplishments. For instance, if my goal was to have a practice that was able to operate without me being on site, and at the time I set the goal I was working five days a week, I would celebrate like crazy when I was able to reduce my treatment schedule from five days to four days.

This is SO simple to do, but it's something I never did. I would say something like, "Sure, four days is good but my goal is zero days at the office." It sounds absolutely crazy, but chances are that you're doing this right now.

Always Celebrate Progress Backwards

One of the first things I teach my clients is how to acknowledge and celebrate their wins by measuring backwards against their previous accomplishments. It is the simplest thing to understand but one of the most powerful things an owner can do to completely alter their mindset from negative to positive, from feeling bad about oneself to feeling good about oneself. The entire Negative Zone concept is about increasing your confidence by acknowledging your wins and celebrating them.

Another big area the Negative Zone concept helps us with, something we all do, is comparing ourselves to others.

What happens when we measure ourselves against someone else's ideals? Another way to say it is what happens when we compare what we have or don't have to someone else? There are only two feelings you're going to have, and neither is very healthy. One, you're going to feel superior to the person you're comparing yourself to, or two, you're going to feel inferior. So, people who always compare themselves to others are swimming around in the Negative Zone. This is where jealousy and envy live. Believe me, I have spent years in this zone. In fact, I still find myself in it from time to time, especially when I start comparing myself to other coaches instead of just focusing on MY progress.

Every time I compare myself to others, my energy stops, momentum halts, and self-doubt creeps in. This is what comparing ourselves to others does to us. Yes, it can be used as a motivator, as long as you are measuring your progress against your own starting point. Otherwise, it's a slippery slope that eventually brings stress, reaction, and low creativity.

One more HUGE tip: People in the Negative Zone LOVE to hang around other people in the Negative Zone. Everyone feeds off of each others' complaints. Choose wisely who you allow into your world. People in the Negative Zone do not make great decisions or choices. They are very reactive to things and make emotionally-based decisions that haunt later on. I've made many of these poor decisions while in the Negative Zone that have cost me hundreds of thousands of dollars.

How do you apply this in your practice? Start by deciding *what* you will measure and what your goal for that is. You need to quantify where you are now, then record your current measurement to establish your baseline. Next, determine the milestones along the way. From there, you can actually measure progress from one point to another.

"Hey, we went from 60 percent utilization to 75 percent. We know we want to be at 85, but you know what, let's celebrate the milestone in the meantime." It's okay to celebrate milestones. It's a must to keep confidence high and momentum moving forward.

Share with Your Staff

I shared the whole Negative Zone concept with my staff and initially they were skeptical (probably like you are now). It was difficult for anyone to share a positive win because the minute they started talking about a positive, it turned into a blaming and a victim party. Always negative. If this happens to you, my advice is this: *be patient.* In my own practice, within the space of just a few staff meetings, the staff started to turn it around and really enjoyed being in a positive place. The conversations in our staff meetings turned from everyone complaining about certain patients or doctors or even negative world events to positive comments. The effect this had on morale and productivity was substantial.

How do I use this concept when I'm with other colleagues?

I try not to put myself in situations where a group of people are talking negatively about the state of health care, reimbursement, or anything of that nature. However, sometimes I find myself in the middle of the conversation. Instead of voicing my views (like I used to do, only to have my words fall on deaf ears), I just politely smile when people talk and quickly remove myself from the negative conversation.

Let me be perfectly candid about this scenario. In my experience, many of the people who are having these conversations are part of the vast majority of owners who are not doing well in their practices. What is worse, they are choosing to stay right where they are. I have no patience for those people and do everything I can to stay clear of them. I highly suggest you do too.

How do you know if you're in the Negative Zone? Be attentive to your mood. Do you feel good about yourself? Are you confident about what you're doing and where your practice is going? These can give you hints about whether you're in or out of the Negative Zone.

Over time, I've become very good about being aware when I'm not feeling good about myself or if my confidence is low. I'll quietly ask myself, "Why is my confidence low?" Many times, just asking the question helps me get out of the Negative Zone. Other times, I'll use podcasts, music, and exercise to escape it. When

I feel that I am in the Negative Zone, I'll pop in my headphones and go for a run while listening to a really good podcast or one of my favorite "get me fired up" songs. Or I'll read a chapter or two in a book I like. If it's a little more dire than that, I'll review my journal and look at all of the wins I've had over the weeks or months. And if it's even more dire than that, I'll call my business coach and ask him for a quick clarity session, which is usually the reason I get into a negative place to begin with—a lack of clarity. I'll speak more on clarity later on in the book.

So, there you have it—those are the two biggest Unfair Advantages that have allowed me to get to the place I'm in and that I know can help you: Active Appreciation and Staying out of the Negative Zone.

I have had conversations over the years with not only PT owners, but entrepreneurs in practically every industry, and all of them have had similar exponential results when incorporating the Active Appreciation and Negative Zone mindsets into their daily habits.

It is an Unfair Advantage because most people don't know about it. However, for the small group of us who do, it has made incredible impacts on our lives, our businesses, and our families. While others continue to struggle and maintain a small vision for themselves, those of us who embrace this type of thinking continue to break through barriers and create futures that are bigger and better than we could have ever imagined.

You now have the power to change your future for the better.

To have different results, one must do things differently. Enjoy being different. Enjoy being unique. The Unfair Advantage concepts have given me the freedom of time and the freedom of money. I have the time to do the things that I love to do on a daily basis and get to enjoy them with the people I love. I am able to take time off from my practice having full confidence in my team, knowing that my practice is going to be better off without me for a few weeks. Join me and be a part of the small group of entrepreneurs in the health care industry who are enjoying the freedom of time, money, relationships, and purpose.

> *"Insanity: doing the same thing over and over again*
> *and expecting different results."*
> **—Albert Einstein**

For more information specifically on Chapter 2, The Unfair Advantage, please visit:

www.TheAutomatedProfessionalPractice.com/book/chapter2.

PART 2

THE FOUNDATION

CHAPTER 3

The Truth About Practice Ownership

Why are most PT practice owners in the uncomfortable position they're in? I feel the answer is obvious: We were educated to be Physical Therapists, not business people. We were taught how to treat patients, document their care, and solve people's physical ailments, but not how to build and grow our practices.

Let me ask you a question:

Were you ever taught business practices in PT school? Things like hiring, marketing, management, and cash flow?

My guess is that besides MAYBE spending a few hours on business in a class one semester, the answer is no.

And guess what? Of course the answer is no. Why? PT schools are not in the business of helping you open up a private practice. They're in the business of helping you pass the boards and become a licensed PT.

Let me ask you another question:

Why did you decide to open up your own practice?

If you're like most PT owners that I've talked to, it probably came down to three reasons:

a. More Time
b. More Money
c. More Freedom

But whatever your reasons, the fact remains that PTs are ill-prepared to manage and operate a successful business.

Now, for those PTs who are deluded into thinking it only requires being a really good therapist to run a practice, let me just say this: Our industry is overflowing with really good PTs who are absolutely unsuccessful in private practice.

So, let's get back to sharing what I learned as I began to rebuild my practice after the fire.

One of the biggest frustrations I had prior to the fire was the lack of time. My time was dictated by everyone—patients, staff, insurance companies—everyone but ME. I never seemed to have a moment to myself to gather my thoughts. I was always in a fog.

What I didn't realize was that I lacked the one thing that was most important to me: time.

I didn't own my time. Actually, my time owned me. And when time owns you, you become very reactive to situations and you have an increased level of worry and stress.

In fact, there's no sense of calmness. Your brain is always on high alert reacting quickly to everything and everyone, which leads to making bad decisions.

This single experience led me to discover **Two Simple Truths**.

The **First Truth** is that we, as independent private practice owners, don't have enough **Time**. We don't have time to manage the practice, treat our patients, and balance some sort of normal family life.

The **Second Truth** I discovered is that PT owners are terrible at delegating. By far, nothing I have learned over the past 14 years as a practice owner and coach of other successful practice owners has been more important to growing a PT practice, while creating an amazing life of freedom of time and money, than **Delegation**. Delegation is merely freeing yourself up from tasks than can be handled by someone else.

When I talk about time, what I am really referring to is **Time Ownership**. How do you know if you own your time or if time owns you? Below is a simple way that I use to help owners clarify if they own their time.

Do YOU own your time?

1. What does your typical weekly schedule look like?
2. Are you focusing on the activities you love?
3. How about activities that give you energy?
4. Do you have scheduled time to think, brainstorm, and strategize?
5. Do you make time to evolve your practice by creating new processes and systems?
6. Do you continue to innovate with better ways of doing things?
7. Do you have scheduled time to focus on your key referral source relationships?
8. Are you able to spend quality time building and deepening important business relationships?

If you've answered no to any (or all) of the questions above, then time definitely owns you. But before your blood pressure shoots up any more, I'm here to tell you that all of that can change.

Here's a great example of how a client of mine, Steve, turned his situation around from time owning him to Steve owning his time.

> "*Time is the only non-renewable, non-replaceable resource we have.*"

When I met Steve, he already had what many would consider a successful PT business. He had two locations, 25+ employees, and was generating over $1.7 million in gross revenue. However, what many people didn't know was that Steve was netting less than $75,000 per year. It was amazing that he was able to keep his doors open.

After a brief conversation, it was obvious that Steve didn't own his time. He wasn't using his time wisely and instead spent most of his time on activities that produced only mediocre or even poor results while draining his energy. He wasn't able to carve out any time for strategic thinking, brainstorming, or process creation, let alone family time. This led Steve to digging a deeper hole of personal and financial despair.

I am proud to say that in just three months after my first conversation with him, Steve was able to turn his financial situation around and was taking home an additional **$9,000 per month**—or just over **$100,000** a year.

So how did he do it?

Steve realized how valuable his time was and how little of it was spent actually thinking about and working on his business. Most of his time was spent treating patients and reacting to staff problems—a cycle of treating and reacting, treating and reacting.

By adjusting his schedule and blocking out time to think, he was able to create some simple, yet effective collection and billing systems. That single step allowed him to solve his financial issues and net an additional $9,000 in profit each month. The simple act of creating blocks of uninterrupted "thinking" time gave Steve the space to see his situation more clearly and work on his business.

Here's the strategy I taught Steve and many other practice owners to help them become more efficient, generate more money, more time, and more freedom.

It's a concept called **bundling**. Most owners have treatment schedules every day of the week. For example, say you see patients Monday through Friday from 7:30 a.m. to 4:30 p.m. During that time you also squeeze in administrative responsibilities, staff and other meetings, as well as marketing for the clinic. Instead, try grouping your treatment hours together in a few long days rather than five average days. For example, if you treat patients four days a week, ten hours per day and give yourself an entire day just to do administrative activities, you'll actually be more efficient. You'll get more done than if you spread the patient care over five days a week, fitting in administrative activities throughout the day.

Why does this work? Studies have found that it takes anywhere from 15 to 25 minutes to reorient yourself to a task once you've been interrupted. When your brain is completely focused on one primary task rather than multiple tasks, the efficiency with which you perform that task sky-rockets; you are "in the groove." Bundling limits the amount of interruptions and allows you to maximize your efficiency.

Focus is the key to getting exponential results. When treating patients, you'll be better off treating all day with minimal interruptions from staff, emails, phones, etc. Just focus on treating and documentation.

If you try adding marketing meetings, staff meetings, or administrative activities into your patient treatment day, the chance of making mistakes or poor, reactive decisions increases, as does your inefficiency as a therapist. You focus on everything else in the clinic EXCEPT the patient in front of you.

Bundling not only helped Steve add $9,000 per month to his bottom line; it has helped me and hundreds of other successful private practice owners increase revenues, decrease our workloads, and streamline our businesses. If you implement this ONE strategy into your schedule, you can expect to see a dramatic increase in how much you get done and how much more money you make.

Without question, the biggest reason why your practice is NOT growing as fast as you would like is due to the lack of delegation on your part. Delegation is not only the secret to Time Ownership, but it's a large part of the success formula for true time and money freedom.

Now, you might be thinking: "How in the world can I *make* more money if I have to *spend* more money hiring staff to delegate things to?"

Or you may be thinking: "I would love to delegate some work to my staff, but the reality is they're not as good as I am."

Or even: "If I delegate all of these things, what in the world am I going do in the practice?"

These are all great questions. The theme of these questions centers around one thing more than anything else: Trust. I realize that many owners have problems trusting their staff. I had the same problems with my staff. I didn't trust that they could treat as well as I did, or communicate with the patients as well, or even handle a potential new patient as well. What I have realized over the years is that trust is built by first, hiring the right kind of people and second, by creating organized systems that produce consistent results.

If you are still hesitant about delegating items to staff, let me help by sharing some answers to the questions above.

Would you agree that in order to grow your practice, you need good people on board to help you? If your answer is yes and your goal is to grow, then you only have one choice: Hire good staff. The bigger concern may be HOW to hire good staff. If that's the case, then the issue is with your hiring process. I'll discuss how to hire and build a great team in Chapter 5.

If you do not delegate because you feel nobody on your staff is as good or capable as you, then my first question is "Why aren't they?" Let's face it, if you're the best at everything in the practice (you're not), you're going to struggle to grow. Simply put, you can only personally handle so many things and still be effective. Your time and energy are limited.

As an owner, you must allow your staff to help. Trust is a result of having confidence in your staff. You must give them the space to perform. Of course, it also helps to have a really great training system. Most likely, you don't have one (at least not one that you use). I'll share my dead simple system later on in the book.

Surprisingly, many owners are unsure of what their role in the practice will be once all their customary duties have been delegated. That's an easy one. You will now have time to actually build a phenomenal practice by leveraging your new-found time to focus on the abundance of opportunities that are out there. Maybe you've always wanted to create a new patient program, develop a product that would help patients, or coach Little League. You now have the time and money to do it.

Let me share a story with you about Becky. Becky is an independent private practice owner in Nebraska. She was a relatively new PT owner when I met her and she was struggling for new patients. After talking with her, it was evident that Becky had time ownership issues and wasn't a big fan of delegation. She felt that her staff couldn't do most of the activities as well as she could.

So, Becky continued to treat patients five days a week, 10+ hours a day. She caught up on her administrative activities on the weekends, barely managing to squeeze in some family time to relax with her husband and two kids—literally between 12 p.m. and 4 p.m. on Sundays. Becky was stressed and her schedule was making it worse. Her relationships with her family and friends started to suffer.

Fast forward five months after we first spoke. Becky had completely modified her weekly schedule using the bundling concept to create more time. She added one full administrative day on Fridays and treated all of her patients in four 8-10 hour days. Her weekends became completely work-free.

What happened next is NOT atypical with Practice Owners who use the bundling strategy.

Becky DOUBLED her new patients and removed 50% of what she calls "unproductive" activities from her plate. Basically, she got rid of the activities that were causing her stress. At the time of writing this book, Becky just celebrated her most profitable month yet ($28,000), is treating patients two days per week, and just hired her third physical therapist. Her practice continues to grow, giving her more time to spend with her family, friends, and horses (she loves horses), all while making more income.

If you're wondering how Becky completely turned around her practice, her financial situation, and her life, you have to look no further than the bundling strategy. This allowed her to create a more efficient treatment schedule, thus freeing up time to get her other administrative work completed, and allowing her to take her weekends back.

The exercise I had Becky go through is actually very simple but as you can clearly see, the results are powerful.

1. I had Becky write down on a piece of paper just one activity that she absolutely didn't like doing or felt was an unproductive use of her time. Usually this is an activity that can be done by someone else at a cost of $10-$20 per hour.
2. Next, Becky wrote down three possible solutions for how she could remove this activity and who she could delegate it to.
3. Next, I had her circle what she thought was the best option.
4. Last, I had Becky write down her next action step that would move this project forward.

Once the activity was fully and completely removed and being successfully handled by someone else, I had her repeat the process.

Now it's your turn.

It's time for you to start getting rid of those pesky activities that you really don't enjoy doing or that you don't do well. My advice is to start with the activities that you really hate that can be delegated to someone else for less than $20 per hour.

Try it. You will love the results.

The Delegation Exercise

1. Write down on a piece of paper just one activity you don't like doing or feel is an unproductive use of your time. Remember, most activities that are wasting our valuable time can be delegated to someone else for less than $20 per hour.
2. Write down three possible solutions to remove this activity and to whom you will delegate it.
3. Circle your best option.

4. Write down the next action step that will move this
   project forward.

For more information specifically on Chapter 3, The Truths
About Practice Ownership, please visit:

www.TheAutomatedProfessionalPractice.com/book/chapter3.

CHAPTER 4

Efficiency Scheduling System

In this chapter, I am going to address how to organize your weekly schedule, how to prioritize your daily schedule, and how to make the most of your time. There are three critical areas that are extremely important in order for you to have the ability to remove yourself from the day-to-day operations of the practice. They are the efficiency of the owner, time management, and the ability to delegate. Before we dive into the owner efficiency system, let me first share what life was like prior to implementing these time savers into my life.

I was always the first one up in the house. Sometimes I would get in a quick workout before work, but many times I valued sleep over exercise. I would go into the kitchen for a quick power bar then head out the door by 7:00 a.m. Most of the time, the rest of the family wasn't even up yet. I usually got to work around 7:15 a.m. and was the first one there. My first patient would arrive at 7:30 a.m. and my day officially started.

It wouldn't take long for the interruptions from the staff to begin.

"Hey Jamey, I have a quick question for you. I have a patient on the phone and they want to know whether you can see them today. What should I say?"

"Jamey, there's a doctor's office on the phone and they need to speak with you about something."

"Jamey, I have the insurance company on the phone, what do you want me to ask them?"

"Jamey, how should I fill out the flow sheet?"

"Excuse me, Jamey, can you sign this?"

Questions and interruptions throughout the day became the normal routine.

I would spend a quick 20 to 30 minutes catching up on phone calls and emails while grabbing lunch. I would have a sandwich in one hand and either my phone or a mouse in the other. It seemed like a never-ending, non-stop boatload of stuff to do.

There's a great saying: *"People who like to put out fires are usually arsonists."* I love this quote by Dan Sullivan because it perfectly described my life at the time. My role was to put out fires all day long. I had no idea that I was also the one setting them.

A typical afternoon for me was not very different from the morning I described. I started treating at 1:00 p.m., fitting in the dreaded documentation any chance I got, and answering staff questions. When a patient was on electric stimulation, I would quickly check my email or grab my phone to see if I missed any calls. My goal was simple: to finish as much work as possible before heading home.

The hard part about this pattern of putting out fires and checking emails on the fly is that I never felt fully present with my patients. I may have physically been there, but I was not mentally present. And the fires were only the beginning; I was worried about my finances, about payroll, whether my employees were happy or not, and if they would leave. I worried about whether a previous patient was not happy with my care. My mind was always somewhere else.

It wasn't always like this. When I first started the practice, I was 100% physically and mentally present. I was right there working with patients, focused and available. However, as the stress of owning a business started to build, the fires grew, and as problems started to arise, I couldn't stay 100% focused on patient care.

By the time my treatment day ended, I was exhausted, mentally and physically. I would finish up with patients around 6:30 p.m. and then complete any notes that I hadn't finished during the day. By the time I left the office I felt like I had just gone through a war. The energy and excitement I once had gave way to exhaustion, worry, and fear. Whatever energy I did have was being given to the office rather than my family.

So of course I felt guilty for not spending more time with my family. This caused even greater stress, but what was I supposed to do? Working long hours and giving everything I had was the only way I knew how to succeed in business.

Unfortunately, my week did not end on Friday. On many occasions, I went into the office on Saturday for a few hours to treat patients, get notes done, or catch up on administrative tasks like bills and mail. This was also a good time to review insurance denials or snoop around the front desk to see what my front desk person was doing (or not doing as was the case many times).

The worst part about going into the office on Saturdays was that I felt good when I left. I was able to get a ton of work done without distractions and felt like I had caught up with the previous week. However, I knew this was a dangerous feeling. Something had to change or I would end up like one of those "Sunday Only Dads." Those are the dads I see with their families only on Sundays because they're working every other day and night.

Today, I work mainly from home. I spend most of my time coaching other business owners on how to grow and create their own self-managed practice. I have time now to think and strategize about my businesses, physical therapy as well as coaching. I'm able to spend time on education, keeping up-to-date on the happenings in the world of physical therapy, and business in general.

I make time for workshops, trainings and conferences. I make it a point to take at least five vacations per year with my family as well as taking at least 100 additional days off from work.

I'm able to operate the practice remotely. I have one management staff meeting per month. The number of emails or phone calls I get from my staff is down to five to seven per week.

When I do go into the office, it's mostly to say hello to the staff, see some of my old patients, and get a sense of the atmosphere in the office. No one bombards me with questions. Some would say that I am lucky, but luck has nothing to do with it.

How did I remove myself from the practice? What's my secret?

The Secret Sauce

I'm going to show you exactly how I did it. Hopefully, you'll be able to grab some of these golden nuggets and apply them to your practice so you can have the freedom to choose your ideal schedule.

One of the first things I did was to address my treatment schedule and how I was utilizing my time. I asked myself if I was using my time as efficiently as possible. Was there a better way? Of course, I realized very quickly that I was not using my time well at all.

I categorized my weekly activities into three major areas: **Treatment Days, Administrative Days, and Free Days**.

Treatment Days

Treatment days, and yes this includes documentation, are when I'm totally focused on treating my patients. That means being fully present, both physically and mentally, and being completely engaged and committed to the patient.

Administrative Days

Administrative days are for all of the other business duties outside of treating and documentation. This includes staff meetings or meetings of any kind, handling bills and other financials, insurance-related issues, and returning phone calls and emails.

I included marketing activities in my administrative days, at least initially. It was easier for me to visit with doctors, do talks, seminars, or events on the days when I didn't have a full schedule of patients. However, later on when I was seeing patients only two days a week, I created an entire day dedicated to growing the practice. I included marketing strategies such as callbacks on this day and left my routine office tasks to administrative days.

Free Days

Free days are time for me to relax, rest, and rejuvenate. For me to be at the top of my game I must have lots of free time. It may sound counter-intuitive to take time off so I can make more money and be more efficient, but it's this type of thinking that has freed me up from my previous life.

I use free days to do the things I love to do—the activities that "fill up my tank." On free days I enjoy playing golf, basketball, and going running with my wife. Free days are the time I use to bond with my kids on family vacations or simply have fun around the house. Just like treatment days and administrative days, free days are about being fully committed and fully present to those activities, keeping my focus on the here and now instead of the worry of the office.

Another concept that goes along with organizing my week is something called the 80/20 rule. To be perfectly candid, it would be nearly impossible for me to have one hundred percent days in those three areas (except for maybe free days). The 80/20 rule allows me to organize my days into what I am going to do 80% of the time.

For example, if I have a treatment day on Mondays, then my focus at the clinic is treating patients. Whether it's an eight hour or even a 10 hour day, my focus is to be fully engaged while treating and getting my notes done. After work, I usually like to spend some time with my kids before they go to sleep and then I unwind. However, I call this a treatment day because 80% of my day was spent treating in the office.

Once I had my days categorized and laid out, I had the freedom to design my work week.

Wow. What a mindset shift. I actually got to design my work week instead of it being dictated by everyone else. After implementing the new schedule, the results were nothing short of mind-blowing. I became significantly more productive in my treatment visits by seeing the same number of clients per week in four days versus five days, and I was also able to complete my notes by the end of the week. Within two weeks of starting this new schedule, I didn't have to go to the office to finish up documentation on Saturdays anymore. Basically, I had freed up another entire day and I could spend Saturdays with my family.

Since I was as productive treating patients four days a week as I was treating five days a week, I decided to use the fifth day as an Administrative Day. I spent the entire day focusing on handling bills and invoices due, as well as finishing up my notes in the rare case I didn't get everything done during my treatment days. I was able to meet with staff on those days, which immediately increased our communication and clarity, boosting their productivity.

Since I was becoming much more efficient, especially with administrative activities, I had time to work on developing and implementing marketing strategies. I spent the first half of my day focusing on administrative tasks like finishing up my notes, checking and responding to emails, meetings, etc. All of the staff meetings as well as any other meetings I had were now scheduled on my Administrative Days.

The second half of the day was for marketing. I scheduled meetings with doctors and other referral sources during this time. Many times, marketing meant time for me to just think and strategize. I created some of my best and most effective new patient referral strategies during this time.

After implementing my new, time-efficient work schedule, my week looked something like this: Monday, Tuesday, Thursday, and Friday were my Treatment Days. Wednesday became a cross between an Administrative Day and a Marketing Day, and Saturday and Sunday became my Free Days. I didn't do any work. I even tried not to think about work. My goal was to fully engage with my family, friends, and fun activities. Was it easy? Not initially. Changing one's habits is never easy, but it sure was worth it.

As I mentioned before, my productivity and efficiency shot through the roof. The number of patients that I personally saw and the number of patients the clinic saw dramatically increased. My stress level, which usually measured around 85 out of 100, started to subside. The feedback I was getting from patients was extremely positive and the number of internal referrals quadrupled.

After my initial disbelief, I realized that this was a direct result of the schedule changes I had implemented. My schedule was more efficient, allowing me time and energy to focus on patients, who in turn rewarded me with more referrals. The energy in the clinic improved as well because the staff felt better about what they were doing due to the increased quality of communication—in spite of the fact that the communication now happened once per week rather than throughout the day every day. I was finally in charge of my schedule. I was finally in charge of my time. Time didn't own me; I owned my time.

As I became more and more comfortable with this schedule, I began to wonder if it was possible to reduce my treatment days down to three a week. That became a reality in less than a few months after implementing the four day a week treatment schedule.

I decided to treat Mondays, Wednesdays, and Fridays with Tuesdays as my Administrative Day. I used Thursdays strictly for marketing. My weekends were still free. I kept this schedule for a while, which allowed me to really grow the practice by putting in place systems and processes that I developed on my non-treatment and free days.

One important note is that in order for me to stay organized, I needed to change how I was using technology. Having sticky notes all over my office wasn't going to cut it any longer. I knew it was time to embrace the world of technology, and that included using my Gmail calendar. Prior to Gmail, I used a paper calendar and lots and lots of sticky notes. I began simply by writing all of my meetings in time slots on the calendar at the beginning of the week. This included work and non-work activities. By the way, this is still how I do it.

Having my schedule laid out graphically allowed me to budget my time and brought order to my work week. I was no longer losing time to putting out office "fires" or reacting to unexpected and seemingly constant interruptions.

Most likely, you are in a state of reacting. You are constantly reacting to something that's happening to you. You're reacting to patients wanting more of your time, reacting to notes that have to be done, reacting to staff interruptions, and many other interruptions which necessitate a response from you. By using your calendar and pre-booking all of your activities for the week, you will create more time and have much more control. Your clarity and focus will increase, giving you more confidence. This is powerful medicine when trying to take your practice to the next level.

At the beginning of each week, in addition to scheduling all my meetings and blocking out time for the week on the calendar, I would also ask myself, "What are the three crucial results I want to achieve this week?" What I can accomplish over a short period of time using this simple idea is still amazing to me. I don't always achieve my desired results every week, but the key is to create a habit of getting your mind focused and in a position to accept these results and achievements. The alternative is remaining distracted by and reactive to the unending minutia.

I suggest choosing simple goals like writing an email to a doctor or other prospective referral source you would like to meet. It could be having an interview with a potential employee. It could be creating your running event program or meeting with your marketing person about holding an event. It doesn't matter what it is. The three results don't have to be grand, and most times they won't be. Many times, the three critical results that I want are small action steps that will lead to the bigger goal.

90-Day Sprints

The final time-efficiency strategy I use has to do with goal-setting and managing projects within the clinic. I call this method of goal-setting 90-Day Sprints, but it also can be looked at as 90-Day Projects. Although I have an overall vision of how I see my practice running and how my life will look in the future,

...e secret to achieving amazing progress is narrowing the focus to 90 days. In my experience and in the books I have read on this subject, 90 days is a perfect amount of time to accomplish many things. It's not so far in the future that it seems unrealistic or remote (like five-year business plans). It's something I can see in the not-too-distant future which will keep me motivated.

At the beginning of every quarter, I make a list of the projects I'd like to complete. It varies from creating relationships with referral sources, to launching a specific marketing plan, to implementing a new weekly time schedule.

A project can consist of anything you want, as long as it's important to you and is aligned with your larger vision. Here's how to do it: Write down the name of each project. Then, write down the end result you want from each project. Finally, write down the next action step that must be taken in order to move this project forward.

Remember those crucial results I spoke about before? The action step should be in line with the project you want to complete in the next 90 days. In essence, your projects will help you determine what you want and need to accomplish each week.

A schedule that allows you to focus on treatment, administrative work, strategic thinking, and marketing, as well as rejuvenating yourself by having fun on your free days, will put you in total alignment with your vision—helping you become significantly more productive and efficient.

Every time I decreased my treatment schedule using the previous concepts and strategies, my business revenues went up significantly. In fact, when I removed myself completely from the treatment schedule, working only three days a week (one Administrative Day and two Marketing Days), my revenues increased by 16%.

The more organized I became and the better I managed my time, the more time I got back. The next step was to leverage my time into more creative and innovative projects that allowed me to exponentially grow my practice.

I know you can do this, too. Begin by organizing your weekly schedule into specific days. Then use a calendar to organize and pre-book meetings and events. Write down the projects you wish to accomplish in the next 90 days. Finally, decide on the three crucial results you want at the beginning of each week.

For more information specifically on Chapter 4, Efficiency Scheduling System, along with helpful, downloadable worksheets, please visit:

www.TheAutomatedProfessionalPractice.com/book/chapter4.

CHAPTER 5

Right Fit Hiring

This chapter focuses on how to attract and hire the best people for your practice. Without a doubt, for me, hiring is the most challenging aspect of being a business owner. It took me a long time and seemingly hundreds of interviews to find the right people for my practice. As you know, if you don't have the right people onboard in your practice, it will be nearly impossible to get to the next level.

A-Players help you leverage and scale your practice. Without the right team, confusion and frustration will be the norm, as I experienced for many years. So, if your goal is to grow, then you only have two choices: grow with the right team or fail to grow without the right team.

For me, hiring the right team started several years into owning my practice when my frustration level was at an all-time high. I asked myself a simple question: "Why is hiring and attracting the right people so difficult?" One of the reasons I came up with was that I wasn't at all specific on who I wanted. Yes, I had a general idea, but I never took the time to write down and describe the perfect person for each position in my company. When candidates showed up for interviews, I tended to react to the person in front of me rather than qualifying the A-candidates right from the get-go. Part of me only cared about filling the position so I could move on to something else. I assumed that people had the same drive, problem-solving ability, and honesty that I had. Boy, was I mistaken.

I had never taken the time to understand the mindset of other physical therapists or given any thought to what their wants and needs were. The bottom line was that I spent so much time making sure the potential employees understood me and how I liked to operate my practice that I never took the time to truly understand them.

Today, when people ask me how I was able to create such a successful practice where I'm able to be off-site as much as I am, I tell them, "I owe it to my incredible team." However, it wasn't always that way.

In the first nine or ten years of my practice, the joke with my friends used to be, "Jamey, who did you fire this week?" or "Jamey, who quit this week?" It seemed like every week someone was quitting or being fired, and someone new was being hired. This went on for years.

I would justify why each of the fifty or so people who came and went in my practice were not the right fit. There was no doubt I had a strong ego. Unfortunately, this ego told me a lot of lies. The biggest lie of all was how it was always the employees' fault that they didn't work out at Schrier PT. It was never mine.

Looking back, having all of these people come in and out of the practice must have cost me hundreds of thousands of dollars in time, money, and wasted potential. The wake-up call came when my most productive PT told me she was leaving. She was a therapist that I genuinely felt I had a connection with and whom I could mentor into an incredible leader. Instead, she left her written notice on my desk one day and two weeks later, walked away without looking back.

This employee's defection affected me more than any other employee who left because I knew she left because of me. I couldn't say she wasn't the right fit because I knew she was. I said to myself, "Wow, this person thought so little of me that she was willing to go somewhere else even though she said that she loved it at Schrier PT." Of course the vague reason she gave me for leaving wasn't the truth because she didn't want to make me feel bad.

That was when it dawned on me that I had created the type of practice I didn't want. It was the type of practice where good people didn't stay; they left because they didn't feel appreciated. A practice where good people who worked hard had very limited opportunities to grow. This was not the vision I once had. I knew that if I didn't change my attitude and my mindset, things were not going to end well. I knew it was already going that way.

The first rule to understanding your employees is this: They care about themselves. It's human nature. Sure, they'll say they care about patients or being a good PT or even about being a team player. However, if you take the mindset that people only care about themselves, it will force you to focus completely on their wants. I never realized it was my responsibility to understand them. It's the same as with patients – my job is to understand them, not the other way around.

This took me years to figure out, but once I realized that I had it all backwards, it took me only minutes to change my approach. I went from a revolving door of hires and fires to a staff (I like to call them my team) of fantastic people. The entire team is engaged and productive. Because I didn't understand my team's needs or perspective, I unwittingly capped their potential. There was no incentive for them to go the extra mile. Who wants to go above and beyond when they aren't appreciated?

Seeing my practice through the eyes of my employees was a game-changer. My new perspective made it all too clear that I was the cause of that revolving door. And I knew that I had to change how I compensated my employees. A paycheck wasn't enough. Employees need an atmosphere where they can grow and contribute, where they feel appreciated and useful. With that in mind, I consciously made an extra effort to appreciate my employees, to give them incentives beyond a paycheck. The atmosphere in the office actually opened up, became more positive, and my team contributed some incredibly valuable ideas to help the practice grow.

That was an important step in building my fantastic team. But a growing practice requires more people. This time around, I wanted to attract the right people and keep them. At the time, I was writing articles and blog posts about business systems and processes. I realized that I didn't have the most important system of them all—recruiting and hiring.

Recruiting-Hiring-Training

When I decided I was going to build a great team, the first thing I did was look at our hiring process. Believe it or not, we did have one, but it wasn't complete. I realized that the hiring process is comprised of three areas: Recruiting, Hiring, and Training.

Recruiting PTs is one of the most challenging areas for any owner. There are far more positions available than there are PTs to fill them. Again, I needed a mindset shift. Instead of focusing on hiring just another person, I looked at the recruiting process as a means to attract the *right candidates*. How was I going to attract the best people? My thought was if I could attract the best applicants, then I couldn't lose by hiring any of them. However, the same goes for less suitable people. If I only attracted these candidates, then basically anyone I hired would be nowhere near the right fit for my company or my vision.

Another huge "aha" I had was that 90% of the time I was looking for an employee out of desperation or reaction. I needed to find a PT or front desk person ASAP because someone had just quit. This type of emotional reaction created a frenzied atmosphere in the practice. Everyone was running around like chickens with their heads cut off trying to fill the position. We were emotionally reacting to someone leaving. Our goal was to get a warm body to fill the position as quickly as possible rather than taking the time to find the right person.

The first thing I did was look at our hiring process

I started by reviewing our open position ad. It was the most generic thing I have ever seen. Do you know how I made my ads? I went on Craigslist and looked at other people's ads, and then I copied and pasted from them. (Sound familiar?)

"Fast-paced and exciting PT office looking for great team player to answer the phones and schedule patients" or "Fast-paced and exciting PT office looking for great team player. We offer great benefits, competitive salary, and a sign-on bonus, etc." Let's face it – I really didn't understand how to write an ad.

The first thing I learned about writing ads is that writing an ad is nothing more than writing a sales letter. How many times had I written a sales letter? Zero. I had to learn not only how to write ads, but how to write sales copy. Whether you want to attract the right employee or more patients to your clinic, the process of writing your ad is the same.

The first thing you need to know is your target audience. Who is that A-player you want? Yes, you have to know what position you're hiring them for, but what other qualities or characteristics does this ideal person have? What role do you envision this person playing in your practice? As the owner, it was my responsibility to be extremely clear about who I wanted in this position.

Hiring a Front Desk Person

I believe the most important person in the practice is the front desk person. It is imperative that they have excellent communication skills. I can't tell you how many offices I've been to in the medical field that have the absolute worst front desk people I've ever met. Seriously, the doctors couldn't have hired any worse. I enter the office and the person says (in a snarky tone), "Hello, can I help you?" I mean, come on, really? I realized that this was exactly who I would end up hiring unless I did something differently.

I wrote down that I wanted a person who has energy, a nice smile, answers the phone like they actually want to speak with you, not like they are trying to get off the phone as quickly as possible. These people do exist, but they're not going to be attracted to an ad that says, "Looking for front desk person, good hours, competitive salary, etc." It's just not going to happen.

What other qualities do you want this front desk candidate to have? Remember, you will be comparing your list of desired qualities and characteristics against the candidates who apply for the position. The clearer the picture of your perfect person, the easier it will be to determine if they are the right fit.

Have you decided what they should wear? At our practice I like to have my front desk person dress in business-casual, looking professional. I don't want them wearing a t-shirt or having lots of piercings, etc. This is what I want. You must decide who you want. Don't make the mistake that I did of trying to duplicate what someone else is doing. It's your practice; it's your vision. There's no wrong answer as long as it is what you want. I'm sharing what I do and why I do it, but don't just do what I do. You've got to figure that out for yourself. This will lead to hiring the right people to help you with your specific business needs and vision.

By far, the best way to attract someone to your practice is

through word-of-mouth. However, a word of caution: If you have bad employees on your team right now, they will attract other bad employees.

A-players will always attract A-players.

Once I started getting rid of these poisonous employees, my good employees felt comfortable referring colleagues they trusted to the practice. Not only do the good employees bring in other good people, they protect your business by keeping bad employees out. The key to word-of-mouth advertising for employees is to have some really good people on board who feel good about bringing on other A-players.

A great way to attract physical therapists is by hosting a student internship program. We would contact local schools and offer to host their students for 10-12 weeks. We specifically asked for students who were either entering or in their third year, and who had a special interest in outpatient orthopedics. Basically, this was a 10-week working interview to determine if they were a right fit candidate. I know many large PT companies do this because of the even greater benefits of getting free labor. That's a great bonus, but more importantly, if the interns do transition to employees, they require very little training since they're already comfortable with our Electronic Medical Records system and other processes.

The Interview

Once you have attracted the candidate, you move into the interview process. When I first started interviewing people, it consisted of one in-person interview, then a decision on whether or not to make them an offer. There was no courting period (like in dating) or "getting to know each other." It was a first-impression decision. I decided to create a multi-step process that allowed us, as well as the applicant, time to determine if we were a good fit for each other.

The interview process was separated into three sections: Phone interview, in-person interview, and the working interview.

I started with the phone interview because there are some spammer applicants, especially on Craigslist. These people literally apply to every position in a certain area, like front desk and PT Aide. They're desperate to find a job so they mass reply to every ad. When we post an ad for the front desk, we typically receive 100-130 applicants. Because of this problem I developed the phone interview process. It's a two-minute phone call where I ask them questions including, "What position specifically are you applying for? We have a few ads on Craigslist, so I just need to know which one you're interested in." The answers I got were amazing. Sometimes it was, "I don't know, what positions do you have available?" I have even had applicants who said, "I'll do anything, what do you need?" Most of the time my response is "Thank you very much, but we do not have that position" and I hang up.

Here's the beauty of the phone interview and how you can quickly determine a potential A-player from a C- or D-player. The applicant responds to your question with this: "I'm applying for the ad you had on Craigslist yesterday about the front desk position for your office in Rockville." Wow, look at the level of detail they just provided. This person is thorough, very clear, very specific, and they know I'm calling for that specific position.

Another benefit to the phone interview is catching people as they really are, not what they want you to see. When I call an applicant about a position, they're not expecting it. This immediately gives me a first impression of their authentic self and ability to communicate. This has been such a time saver, especially with front desk people whose resumes sounded good, but their communication skills did not match their resumes.

Prior to the phone interview, the candidate would put their best foot forward during the in-person interview and many times seemed great. They said the right things, they were all dressed up, and they communicated well, almost as if they had read *How to Communicate During an Interview*. Later on, once they had the job, they started speaking a little differently and being rude to patients and staff. I realized later that their presentation during the interview was a façade and their true nature was now coming out. Once discovered, I had to fire them and start over. This cost me time and money, and filled the company with negative energy.

I can't tell you how many times I would call and say "Hello, can I speak with Liz, please?" and get the response "Yeah, who's calling?" I would continue, "This is Jamey Schrier. I'm calling from Schrier Physical Therapy about a position she applied for." Then the tone would quickly change. "Oh, hi. How are you doing?" They would immediately become really nice and kind. Then I would ask, "Hey, I just wanted to call and ask you—we have a few positions available, which one in particular were you applying for?" Their answer to this would determine whether I hung up or kept asking questions.

If they were genuine and consistent with their resume, the call went something like this:

Me: "Hi, is Liz there?"

Liz: *"Yes, this is Liz. Who's calling please?"*

Me: "This is Jamey from Schrier Physical Therapy. Do you have a few minutes to talk?"

Liz: *"Sure I do."*

Me: "Great. I wanted to know what position you were applying for."

Liz: *"I was applying for the front desk position that you posted yesterday on Craigslist."*

Me: "Perfect. When would be a good time for you to come in for an interview?"

I could tell right away from their responses that they had passed the phone interview test. Sometimes I would add an additional question like "Why did you apply for this position with our company?" Again, I am more interested in the way they handle the question than the specific answer they give. I care more about character first, then skills. The phone interview was designed to weed out the people whose resumes looked good, but who didn't match what was written on their resumes. This is when having a very clear understanding of the type of person you want for each position becomes extremely important.

The In-Person Interview

First, absolutely every applicant must fill out and sign an application form. The one we use is fairly standard but does the trick. By signing the application, they are telling you the information they have given is accurate and truthful. It protects you as the owner in case they "misinform" you. This should be done BEFORE the in-person interview process.

As for the "salary desired" portion, have them fill it out. If they're not sure, be careful as to why they're not sure. Did they not do their homework before applying for the job? I want people who are upfront and honest. Everybody knows the "going rate" for a position. It may not be what you're willing to pay, but at least you know they did their homework and are serious about their next position.

The most important change I made when performing in-person interviews was to start including one of my A-players in the interview. I personally always choose an A-team member who has the same or a similar position to the position I am filling. For those of you who have very small practices and may not have the luxury of using a staff member, try asking someone outside the practice to sit in. As long as you trust their judgment, it's always better to have a second opinion. I had my wife help me with interviews until I had a good employee whose judgment I trusted.

The biggest challenge I had when I conducted interviews on my own was always to want to hire the person immediately. I was easily influenced and impressionable because I was trying to check this off my list of "things to do." I really didn't appreciate the importance of it. My approach was to get them to like me and want to be a part of my team. My interview consisted of me doing most of the talking rather than the candidate.

What kind of questions should you ask during the interview? To be perfectly candid, I don't believe the type of questions you ask is the most important aspect of the interview. In fact, most of my questions are quite basic. You can find them on the Internet just by typing **interviewing questions** into a search engine. My number one objective is to get them talking.

My most effective question to get candidates talking is: "What specific previous experiences can you share that will demonstrate why you will be very successful at Schrier PT?" The key words are *specific* and *experiences*.

I've found the best way to predict how well someone will do is to look into their past experiences. For instance, if you are hiring a marketing person who is outgoing and has the ability to communicate well with others, then ask them to give you examples of how they have demonstrated these qualities in other positions or in their life. For example, ask if they have run events in the past, perhaps for a school or church group. It matters less what their examples are and more that they relate them specifically to the job description for the position. This is one of the reasons it becomes very important for the owner to take the time to write down clearly who they want, including characteristics and skills.

Let me share an example from an interview I had with a candidate for a marketing position. The candidate didn't have any direct marketing experience for a PT practice or any other health care-related business. However, she did have experience organizing and running a huge event for young women. Now, was there a difference between organizing a church group event and being the marketing director responsible for visiting doctors' offices and arranging race events? Yes, but the differences were small and I knew she was coachable. I ended up hiring her and within a few months she doubled the referrals to our practice. My advice is to include questions that will elicit the candidate's life experiences during the in-person interview. As long as they're coachable and hungry for the position, they have a strong potential to become a great hire.

At our practice, we had always done working interviews for our Physical Therapists, but never for other positions. Currently, we include working interviews for every single position in our company. The other thing we added was having an **active working interview** versus a **passive working interview**. The difference between the candidate just standing there watching (passive), occasionally nodding their head, versus having them fully engage is the difference between night and day.

In the past when we have a front desk candidate do their working interview, the candidate would sit right behind the front desk staff member and watch. The candidate would occasionally ask a question, but most of the time they sat silently while the front desk person did all of the talking. Now, it is all about having the candidate get engaged. Once the candidate was taught the correct way to answer the phone, the next phone call was theirs. It was "do or die" time. Either they had what it takes and it was natural for them or it wasn't. Obviously, we gave them more than one chance, but when you add up all of the other areas of the front desk, it was easy to decide whether they were the right fit A-player we were looking for or not.

Doing a working interview also gives the front desk candidate a tangible, hands-on experience of what the position is going to be like.

When you combine the short phone call, the in-person interview, and the working interview, you will have a clear idea of whether or not this person is the right fit for your practice. The hardest decision may be choosing between two great candidates. That's a decision we all wish we had every time.

> **What I have learned is this: be very upfront with your offer. Have everything in writing.**

Now comes the difficult part for most owners and what was definitely a challenge for me: the offer. When I used to discuss the offer during the interview, I was so ill-prepared that I was literally giving answers "off the cuff." My answers were too general because I didn't put any time into preparing and thinking about what the other person wanted. I would say things like, "Well, I don't know what our salary range is, what are you looking for?" Every interview was different. Nothing was systematic or consistent. My goal was to find out what they were looking for in terms of salary, benefits, CEUs, etc. I would just say, "We're competitive with everybody else," but the reality was that we didn't have our act together, and it showed. I guarantee we lost some good candidates because they knew we weren't organized. And I know for a fact that people want consistency and predictability. Why? Because that equals low risk and most employees want low risk, guaranteed employment with little change, if possible. It took me years to learn that this is what they wanted, because my thinking was completely opposite, focused on me, not them.

What I have learned is this: be very upfront with your offer. Have everything in writing. If you're not sure, tell them "I'm not sure."

One of the key questions I ask just prior to the offer question is: "If we were sitting here two years from now and we were to look back on today, what would have to happen for you to be completely happy with your professional life?" There are many ways to ask this question, but the real purpose of it is to determine whether they see themselves going somewhere or becoming more than what they are now. Do they have a bigger future in this profession or are they more interested in a being a regular PT who looks forward to yearly reviews so they can get a three percent raise? If they have no aspirations beyond where they are now, then they cannot join my team. Period. I don't care whether they're a PT, Senior PT, or PT Aide. No future, no job. You decide what works best for you and your practice, but hiring an employee who just wants a paycheck and has no goals for themselves is a recipe for disaster.

Before leaving the in-person interview (or it can be after the working interview), I know exactly what the prospective employee wants. There's no confusion or misunderstanding. Unless they have misled me (and that does happen sometimes), I can now create an offer letter in good faith, knowing I am in the ballpark of what they want. This greatly reduces the back-and-forth negotiations that tend to happen when there is little understanding between both parties, especially on the major areas like salary, health insurance, paid time off, bonuses, and CEU money. Of course, there might be other areas of interest like disability insurance, but these are the big ones.

If you have done your part and have taken the time to create a comprehensive job description, salary or hourly range per position, benefits for the company, bonus system per position, and vacation time, you will be very comfortable when negotiating and discussing the specific details. Otherwise, you may be like I was and get caught up in the emotion of it all and start changing the benefits on the fly. DON'T DO IT. The only employees you will attract are BAD employees.

Here's one example of an interview I had after I did everything perfectly. It was for a physical therapist staff position and we started talking specifics.

PT: *"Jamey, I absolutely love your practice, I definitely want to come work here."*

Me: "Great, I'll send you an offer letter that will be what you are asking for."

PT: *"Perfect."*

I always include a time limit on the offer—a date that indicates when the offer will expire. I do this because I want a yes or a no. I hate when things don't have closure. If they want you and you want them, it should be a no-brainer. After five days (my offer was good for two days), I heard back from the PT.

PT: *"Your place was great, but I took another job."*

Me: "Why?"

PT: *"Oh, your offer was too low."*

The reason I tell you this story is because this is the reality of working with people. You can do everything right and the person still doesn't end up working for you. However, this process has significantly reduced the number of poor hires, allowed me to create a system that my Clinical Directors now use, and saved me a huge amount of time and money.

More often than not, once I had sent an offer letter (which was really just putting in writing what we already had discussed), I usually received a personal call saying the candidate was in or

I would get a question. At least the process kept moving, versus being in purgatory without knowing what they were thinking.

As long as there is continuing communication, the hiring process is working.

The other piece of advice I will share based on my experience is that you must be prepared to walk away. Be prepared, no matter how great you think the person is, to say, "I don't think you're the right fit for us." If you're unsure about someone, go with a no. I have never been unsure of A-players, only people who turned out to be B- or C-employees. Uncertainty is your gut telling you they are NOT an A-person.

> *As long as there is continuing communication, the hiring process is working.*

The opposite is also true. Many times an employee will ask for significantly more than you are willing to give them. The "old" Jamey would have ALWAYS walked away. However, sometimes A-players know their worth and value to the company and are prepared to clearly demonstrate why they are worth the investment. If their performance history is legitimate, then you will want to strongly consider bringing them on board.

The late Steve Jobs wrote in his autobiography, "Hire A-plus people." A-plus people will always generate ten times more value to the company than a B- or C-employee. Don't let the salary number scare you, as long as they can show you how you will achieve your ROI (return on investment).

This was another topic that I didn't fully understand that kept me trapped in my clinic for so long. For many years, I was so money-conscious. However, what I should have been was investment-conscious. I looked at every employee as an expense on my profit and loss statement, much like a CPA would. WRONG THINKING. One of the colossal mistakes I made, and one that I see owners making, is viewing their employees as expenses instead of investments. The difference is huge. Not only are your employees not an expense, they're your greatest asset. And what do we do with assets? Invest. With expenses or costs, the goal is to minimize them. However, with investments, the goal is to maximize your return. Even if you're paying someone $100,000 a year, the real question you, as an owner, should be asking is: "What is my return on investment going to be and how long will it take? Is it $300,000, $400,000, $500,000 in return or is it $150,000?"

Again, if you start looking at your staff as investments then you will appreciate finding an A-plus person who is asking for more money, because they will bring with them ten times more value. A C-level person may want less money but might only bring in two times more value. My advice is to go with the proven commodity and invest more money.

The Hiring Phase

The hiring phase has officially started when the candidate formally accepts the written offer by signing their name. In my practice, the hiring process is nothing more than a series of steps, a checklist of exactly what needs to be done and by whom.

Please download your FREE copy of The Hiring Checklist at www.TheAutomatedProfessionalPractice.com/book/hiringcheck-list. This will be helpful for the next section.

You can have as many people involved in the hiring process as you choose. In my practice, I have myself, the clinical director, the administrative assistant, the payroll person, and my marketing director, who also handles the IT role of adding the new employee to our website and giving them an email address.

The most important aspect of the Hiring Checklist is obvious—it has all the necessary steps of the process written down in one place. For us, this includes reviewing the handbook, filling out the information for legal and payroll forms as well as being added to payroll. There is also adding them to our health insurance plan, our Electronic Medical Records system, and filling out the in-network applications for Blue Bross Blue Shield and Medicare. In our hiring process, I include the training process the employee must complete within the 90-day introductory period. We do background checks for credit and personal history. We also use personality testing to help identify the ideal candidate for the position we are hiring. Obviously, if anything negative comes up during the background check or any of the testing, then we'll have to deal with it. However, this hasn't happened yet.

The Hiring Checklist's greatest value comes from keeping everyone organized and keeping us from missing something. I can remember that on at least one occasion, one person thought someone else was going to do the new employee's application for Medicare, and we found out a year later that the PT still wasn't credentialed. I can't tell you how much money not having a PT credentialed with Medicare cost us. All fixed with a simple checklist.

As far as who should do what with regard to the checklist, it is completely up to you. I am very big on choosing the best person to handle a specific task regardless of whether it is their "job" or not. Many times, some people just don't have the natural skills to complete a task in a simple way. Assigning the best person for each task really seemed to help everyone work together to bring on an employee without any significant issues.

One warning: DO NOT have your name next to too many steps. In fact, do whatever you can to have your name next to as few steps as possible. My name is not next to any step individually. I am on a few steps with my administrative assistant (who is off-site) as a go-to person in case there is a question or problem. When an employee is interviewed and hired, I am as close to hands-off as possible, unless they are a Director who reports directly to me.

Every person involved in the hiring process has access to the forms and handbook via a Dropbox folder. We make sure every person involved in the process has access to the folder in order to make it super simple to complete their steps. We've stopped making tons of packets and only print out what is needed. This saves time and clutter. Nothing is missed, from ordering business cards to getting a Schrier PT polo. All of these things are very organized and very simple. It's amazing how much this checklist has reduced stress on us and the new employee.

You may be wondering why I am not more involved in my hiring process. After all, it's my name on the door and I should know who is coming in and out of the company. I look at the hiring process as nothing more than a series of tasks. As you know, any qualified person can execute a task if they are trained and it is clear what the result should be. I am completely in the loop of the process because I am cc'd on most emails. As far as not knowing who comes into the practice, I personally introduce myself to every employee and engage in a little small talk. I also read their resume, application, Kolbe test (our version of a personality test), and any other relevant forms to get a feel for the person. I must admit, I only do this for therapist hires. I completely trust my Clinical Directors in hiring front desk staff and PT Aides.

My role is to be a mentor and coach to my direct reporters (i.e., Directors). We have an understanding that I am here to help them talk through the problem or issue and provide advice and feedback. My role is NOT to do it for them. I have made that mistake many times, never giving my Directors a chance to shine. I'll discuss more on delegation in later chapters.

Training

Now that the hiring paperwork is completed, it's time to focus on training. More specifically, helping the new hire get up to speed in how we do things at Schrier PT and making certain they are doing it to our standards.

The problem I used to have with training new staff was that I never really put a lot of thought into exactly how I wanted people to behave in each position. In addition, I didn't have a clear measure that indicated if the team member was performing well in the position or not. Most of my energy was zapped by my anxiety, or being overwhelmed with everything else going on in the practice. I didn't have much time to spend thinking about training systems. What I failed to realize until years later was that there was NOTHING more important to my practice than having a properly-trained team member who was achieving the desired results.

The flip side of having properly-trained employees is having completely untrained employees, or worse, trained by their previous employers. Of course, my hope was that they came with awesome training without the need for me to have to train them. Unfortunately, the hard truth was that if I didn't train my staff, I was relying on someone else to have trained them. After several years of doing it this way and getting poor results from my employees, I decided it was time for a change. I created staff training systems for every position in my company.

I began by writing down what I wanted from each position, how I envisioned each position would operate, and developed metrics to show the expected performance, including the targets I expected an employee to hit.

For example, I expect the front desk person to have a cancellation/no-show rate under 8%. If we had scheduled 100 patient visits in a week and we saw 93 of them, then the cancellation rate would be 7%. For my Physical Therapists, the expectation is to treat 63 visits a week.

This type of specificity, although initially uncomfortable for me, was exactly what was needed to reduce any confusion among the staff. With that said, our employee training systems not only helped them meet or exceed their productivity targets, it also helped them understand how to do it in a manner that was consistent with the company's vision and culture.

In essence, as the owner, you're painting the canvas with the picture of how you want your practice to look, feel, and operate. This is one of the most important areas in which an owner can spend his/her time. Ask yourself "What does my picture look like once an employee has completed their training?" For instance, if it's a front desk person, how do you want them to answer the phone? Schedule a new patient? Communicate with your Physical Therapists? Schedule out the plans of care? Are they expected to do confirmation calls for patients? What kind of reports are they supposed to generate and by what day? Whatever it is that you want from them, it must be clearly communicated, written out, and included in their training. The results will come directly from how well they are trained.

In my company, we have a Training Checklist. This way, it's very easy to have an employee trained to perform the activity satisfactorily and have the trainer initial beside the task indicating competence. At first, this can be a time-consuming task. My recommendation is to enlist the help of some of your A-players who are already in the position. Let's face it; they know how the position should be done better than you. Ask for their help.

Here's the beautiful part: Once you've done it, you don't have to do it again. You can (and should) modify your trainings from time to time, but the bulk of the training material is done.

As I mentioned previously, our training checklist must be initialed by the person who is responsible for training the new team member on that particular task. (Sometimes we have different people train them depending on their expertise.) When a trainer initials an area, this means the employee is completely competent in performing that task. When a front desk trainee answers the phone, they are considered competent when it is performed the way we expect them to do it. It is either a "yes—competent" or a "no—needs more training." This is very straightforward and duplicatable.

To wrap up this section, I discussed and shared a lot about recruiting and the way we do it to consistently attract A-players. We discussed the difference between recruiting and hiring, and how using a simple checklist can make this process easy. Finally, I shared how a good training program can elevate the productivity and efficiency of an employee quickly. The best part is it can be performed by another person on your team so you can focus on other things while your staff continues to attract superstar A-players.

For more information specifically on Chapter 5, Right Fit Hiring, please visit:

www.TheAutomatedProfessionalPractice.com/book/chapter5.

CHAPTER 6

Delegation Made Easy

This chapter is absolutely critical for owners who would like to confidently and permanently move unproductive activities and tasks off their plate. In addition, owners will learn my secrets for balancing time between home life and work life.

Unfortunately, many owners feel trapped in their practice, unable to manage the various tasks that overfill their days. The result is that they stay late and work long hours, sacrificing quality time with the people they love the most.

If an owner can learn how to delegate activities or tasks, leveraging their time becomes infinite and the sky is the limit on what can be accomplished. However, the opposite is also true for owners who remain fixated on doing everything themselves. Time, instead of an ally, becomes the enemy. There is never enough time in the day and the time they do have is spent on boring and non-energizing activities.

This was me several years ago when I started this journey. I was frustrated and anxious, confused and not confident. I was never sure of any decision I made, always fearful that I had made a bad decision.

My entire attitude changed after the fire. Once I became totally clear and committed to the idea that I wanted to have a "real" business, not just a job working 60-70 hours a week, my vision suddenly changed. I was clear on what a real business would look like. To me, it was a practice that didn't require me to be there six days per week. The practice could run on its own for a period of time with a staff that I could trust. That vision grew and evolved into the Automated Practice.

I felt owning this type of practice would give me the freedom and flexibility to give patient care as much or as little as I wanted. It would also allow me to take more time off and go on vacations with my family. Finally, I knew there was more for me than just owning a small practice. Don't get me wrong... I was proud of my accomplishments and grateful for the opportunity to help others, but I always felt that if I had the time, I could create something more directly in line with my purpose and natural ability.

Fast forward ten years. Currently, I have a profitable practice with two locations that operate without me on site. I have an amazing staff that is empowered and encouraged to do what they feel is right. This newfound freedom has allowed me to create a one-of-a-kind, high-level coaching program that helps other private practice owners simplify their practices to allow them more time to create an exciting life.

So, that is a little taste of the power of delegating and how it has changed not only my life, but my kids' lives, my staff's lives, and the lives of the clients I now serve. Let's begin.

The Ego

When it comes to business, I feel that we operate within two types of ego. We have an ego that I consider a good ego and, of course, a bad ego. The good ego, for example, was that voice that encouraged us to open up our practice. This ego gives us that vision and confidence that tells us, "I want to do this on my own. I want to have my own practice, make my own hours, make my own rules, and get paid more money. I want to treat people the way I feel they should be treated and to be home with my family when I want."

That's the good ego, the one that helps us overcome risk and fear. It says, "I'm doing this." The good ego gives us confidence, inspiration and motivation. Many times, however, once we open up our practice, there's another ego that takes over our brains. It's the bad ego. This ego tells you that because this is YOUR practice it's up to YOU to do everything. Now, initially you may have to perform a lot of activities other than treating patients. However, over time, this ego won't let go of these activities. This ego wants us to do it all. The bad ego prevents us from letting go, and letting go is the only thing that will give us freedom. I believe that this is why most practice owners don't grow and expand. It's definitely why it took me years and years to finally let go. My bad ego refused to let go of activities, making it seem like I was the only person who could do them. This ego is really good at enlisting fear to help keep everything the same. The mantra is "change is bad" if it means letting go.

Controlling that ego allowed me to create my automated PT practice. Although it took me years to confront the bad ego and put a choke hold on it, other practice owners that I train are doing it in weeks. They're creating awesome practices and positively impacting their communities, while having the freedom to enjoy it all.

Rule #1 for confronting your bad ego: Use Radical Honesty. We have to be honest about what is currently on our plates. This is extremely important, because many owners like to justify why they do a particular activity that could (and should) be delegated. Rather than being completely honest, they immediately begin to tell themselves why they can't get rid of it. This further reinforces and justifies the need for keeping the activity. The result is that they don't let go of it.

The Activity Organizer

If you're ready to begin letting go of the things that are holding you back, then let's go through an exercise that has worked for me and many others. It is called The Activity Organizer™. *To download your FREE copy of The Activity Organizer, go to* www.TheAutomatedProfessionalPractice.com/book/activityorganizer.

Step One: The first step is to list all the activities and tasks that are currently on your plate. For instance, treating patients is an activity. You want to write that one down. Next is documentation. You can't treat without documenting it. Treating and documentation is universal among most practice owners. Treatment and documentation is what all PTs have in common. When I did this exercise, my list consisted of activities such as answering phones, scheduling patients, getting heat packs, answering staff questions, calling patients back, turning on machines, getting patients on/off exercise equipment, bookkeeping, and many others.

What activities do you do in a typical work week?

The best results happen when you are as specific as possible. Don't make the same mistake I did and get caught up in justifying why you're doing these things when you're writing them down. Stay focused. Just write!

Step Two: Once you have written down all of the activities you do in a given week, the next step is to determine if the activity gives you energy or not. In other words, do you really enjoy doing it? Remember, there are no right or wrong answers. It's whatever is true for you. I hated bookkeeping, so I wrote down "L" for Low Energy next to bookkeeping on my list.

This is where the voice of the bad ego can make this process difficult. At the time, I felt I could use QuickBooks to do bookkeeping. Did I truly love it? Did I get tons of energy from my bookkeeping duties? The honest answer was no. My advice is to trust your gut on this. In all honesty, I began to question how much I really enjoyed treating. I initially put it in the high energy category, but as I thought about it more and analyzed how I felt, I realized that I only enjoyed working with certain types of patients. I wrote specifically the type of patients that gave me energy in the high energy category and the other ones in the low energy category. The more specific you can be with the low energy activities, the easier it will be to remove the activity later on.

Another activity I hated was documentation. Yes, I know we legally have to do it, but I still put it in the low energy category. Being interrupted with questions from the staff was a very negative task for me. However, once I thought about it more, I realized that I enjoyed helping my staff problem-solve and being a resource for them. However, I didn't like the manner in which it happened. So, I split the activity into high and low energy and wrote specifically what I liked and didn't like.

Marketing is another complicated activity. Many owners group all marketing activities into one big bucket. Of course, a marketing activity can range from visiting with a doctor to creating a campaign for runners to helping a patient refer her brother into the clinic. When it comes to marketing, I suggest separating out all of your marketing projects. Most practice owners hate marketing in general, but when they consider specific activities, many realize they enjoy some aspects of it. This exercise will also help you understand and see your marketing strategies clearly.

When writing down your high energy and low energy activities, do not be surprised if you have very few high energy activities compared to low energy activities. When I first went through this exercise, 90% of the weekly activities, tasks, and duties I was doing were in the low energy section. No wonder I was anxious all the time while getting less than optimal results.

The main point of this exercise is to first be aware of what you're currently doing and where your time is being spent, then delegate these low energy tasks to someone else.

If you're like me and look at your business as a game, then the game is all about removing low energy activities from your plate. That's it. All progress, money, time, and freedom will come from focusing on how to remove things you don't like and doing the things you do like. This simple idea is the most powerful concept I have learned. To this day, I continue to remove activities I don't like and delegate them to someone else.

Step Three: Now the fun part—delegating. The first activity I picked from my low energy list was bookkeeping. My personality was not detailed enough nor was my knowledge strong enough to keep consistent, well-managed financials.

In order to remove something from your workload, you have to be clear about the result you expect. The question to ask is "What is the desired result?" I have spoken a lot about clarity in previous chapters, and it will continue to come up throughout the rest of the book. If we are not very clear in our own minds about the result we expect, we cannot communicate our intentions to anyone else. Instead, we will create confusion and teach indecisiveness—two traits that destroy a practice.

It took me nearly an hour to clearly write down exactly what I wanted from the person who ended up taking over bookkeeping. I wanted expenses to be accurately entered in the appropriate category, bills to be prepared in a timely fashion, profit/loss statements to be completed monthly, a yearly budget done by month, and several other things.

My clarity regarding financials became so sharp that my confidence immediately increased even before I hired someone to take it over. Just the thought of someone else doing this activity properly helped me relax and focus on finding the right person. I went to Google, typed in "small business bookkeeping" and narrowed my choices down to three. I interviewed them by phone and hired the person I thought could provide me with what I wanted.

Within 90 days, my new bookkeeper, who I hired as a consultant, not an employee, took over all of the financial tasks. She added so much more value than I ever expected, because this was her passion and her expertise.

Do you know what the most difficult part about delegating this activity was? MAKING A DECISION. The mental gyrations and the back-and-forth I did for literally months was more stressful than actually doing it.

I didn't realize how large a stress factor it was until it was removed. And I never thought for one second, "I want this back." That's how you really know if it's a low energy activity. If you move something off your plate and want it back, then it is either your bad ego talking or it's probably a high energy activity for you. In the latter case, you can take that task back and choose a different low energy activity to delegate.

I took something extremely important to my practice and delegated it in fewer than 90 days using this exercise. My goal after that was simple... repeat the process for every low energy activity I had written down. My focus became crystal clear as I continued to look at each low energy activity in every area of my practice and figured out how to get rid of it completely and permanently.

Could you imagine having practically every low energy activity removed from your workload and given to someone who could do it better? What would that do for you personally—your physical energy, mental energy, and creative energy? Imagine the impact it would have on your relationships with patients, staff, your spouse, and your kids.

To this day, I have not found anything more powerful that

has affected my life, my income, and my relationships more dramatically than this exercise of delegation.

Using Technology in Delegation

One of the questions I constantly ask myself is: "How can technology help me remove this activity or improve the outcome?" Prior to hiring my bookkeeper, I was paying bills using paper checks, filing invoices into paper folders, and housing them in the storage office in my clinic. I knew this process was inefficient, but I wasn't sure how to fix it. Luckily, my bookkeeper did. I constantly asked her how we could do things faster, easier, cheaper, and simpler (F-E-C-S). I used her expertise to improve my practice and leverage my time.

Her only hesitation was that most of her clients were not open to change, especially when it came to technology. I made it clear to her that I was not only open to it, but expected her to push her own boundaries by questioning what she currently used. If she could help me do things F-E-C-S, then it would help her other clients, too.

The results of just some of the technological upgrades we made in bookkeeping:

- Stopped using paper printouts of financials. Everything became electronic.
- Stopped mailing out payments and began paying bills online using a company (bill.com). I now spend less than five minutes per month paying bills compared to three to four hours, saving over 42 hours in time per year.
- The bookkeeper had secured access to my accounts that allowed her to reconcile and question any non-approved charge.
- She had also secured access to my credit card statements

online, which made it easier to enter the charges into the appropriate account.

Later on, I increased the role of bookkeeper to include functions that typically a CFO would perform but at a fraction of the investment. This included:

- Access to my EMR system to easily balance collections from patients and insurance companies with what was being deposited.
- Handle staff bonuses.
- Update my simple financial dashboard monthly and communicate with clinical directors.

I don't know for sure how much time I saved having the bookkeeper do all of these activities for me, but I can say that I wouldn't be spending the large amount of time with my family while making significantly more money if I didn't do it. I used to stress about money and financials all of the time. Now, I am at peace knowing I have someone who is on top of things.

As I mentioned earlier, the most difficult part of this entire delegation process was deciding to do it. It was so easy to come up with reasons and justifications to not let go. I used to tell myself all sorts of things, about why I had to keep doing an activity. Although this wasn't the case for me with bookkeeping, it was in many other areas of the practice... like patient care.

I came to the conclusion that if someone else could do the activity at least 80% as well as I could, and it was on my low energy activity list, then I was okay with delegating it. The other challenge that came up was with the employee who I was delegating the activity to. The objections I got either had to do with being somewhat confused about what I wanted specifically or that the additional activity would add more to their already busy schedule.

Once I was clear on what I wanted, it became rather easy to communicate it to them. If I wasn't completely clear, it caused more confusion for the employee and more frustration for me.

Delegation was also instrumental in creating some of the awesome processes we have at Schrier PT. Once I communicated to the employee why they were going to begin taking over an activity, many times they had questions about how to do it. This led to re-examining the existing process (as we did in the bookkeeping example) and improving it. By using the F-E-C-S question, the employee and I could brainstorm about how to create a better, more efficient system. However, once I decided that this activity was going to be taken off my plate, at no time did I even *think* about taking it back.

Some typical objections that came from this were:

1. How to handle patient objections with scheduling out full plans of care.
2. How to collect co-pays and co-insurances at the time of the patient visit.
3. How to handle cancellations and no-shows.

In each case, we established systems to handle the individual situation. But ALL of these systems started with first deciding to delegate the activity. I fully believe that had I not decided to delegate these low energy activities, I would have never created the systems in my practice that allowed me more freedom over my schedule and finances.

Staff Meetings

I'd like to talk briefly about staff meetings. One way to ensure that your team is on the same page with you is with regular staff meetings. We hold weekly staff meetings in each of our clinics, but some owners choose every other week. I wouldn't do less than bimonthly because of the momentum and rhythm meetings have on an office.

My staff meetings used to be a waste of time. It was 60 minutes of me talking about whatever was on my mind. At the time, I felt like it accomplished a lot, but later on I realized it was a waste of everyone's time.

Once I began delegating, staff meetings became one of the best ways to learn how each activity was progressing. Owners need constant communication. This helps us increase our confidence in our staff, which encourages us to delegate even more activities.

It's amazing how many owners, especially those with smaller practices, don't have consistent staff meetings. Having consistent staff meetings is incredibly important to a practice's success. In addition to weekly staff meetings, we have monthly and quarterly management meetings. This allows us to stay in personal communication. When there is a problem, I know that it will be communicated and hopefully addressed within a week, versus hearing about it months later, costing time and thousands of dollars.

Here's the format of our meetings:

1. Share our successes or wins from the previous week.
2. Review the key metrics for each position.
3. If metrics are below target, discuss why and create a plan of action.
4. If metrics are above, celebrate.
5. Any housekeeping matters.

That's it.

The unique thing we do at our practice and something I teach my private clients is *Active Appreciation*™. It's so easy to get caught up with the negativity and problems of the practice (and the world). So, I make it a focus to start off our meetings sharing only positive things that happened in the previous week. This increases everyone's energy and it's fun.

The next thing we do is review metrics. Clarity in a practice begins with an objective measure. Each area of my practice has metrics that determine if we're achieving our stated goal. Too many times I wondered how a particular area was doing. I would spend valuable time worrying about whether my front desk people were taking care of the patients the way I expected. Now, instead of worrying, we have metrics like cancellation rates, no-show rates, and collections rates to determine whether the work is being done properly.

Establishing metrics for each area of the practice and having a time where the person in charge can communicate those metrics (i.e., staff meeting) will absolutely improve your numbers. I recall that within two weeks of having weekly staff meetings and having the front desk person report her numbers, our cancellation rate went from 15% to less than 10%. That represented $3,000 per week in direct additional revenue.

Sharing numbers empowers staff and increases accountability. The best part of this type of staff meeting is that it only lasts 20 minutes versus 60 minutes. Monthly and quarterly meetings last longer because of the nature of the conversations, but each manager reports his/her metrics just like the weekly staff meetings.

This is my secret to running staff meetings. We allow people to report their numbers, either congratulate them on a job well done, or collaboratively help them improve the metric for the next week. Of course, this is done in a non-threatening manner, but my team understands that it is important that they turn any shortfall around as soon as possible.

The purpose of this chapter was to share with you not only how I delegate activities, but why delegation is vitally important to growing a practice, creating balance, freedom, and money. Over the years I've realized that if you choose to not implement any of the ideas I have shared thus far and only focus on getting low energy activities off your plate, you will still create a more profitable practice and live a happier life.

For more information specifically on Chapter 6, Delegation Made Easy, please visit:

www.TheAutomatedProfessionalPractice.com/book/chapter6.

CHAPTER 7

Measure for Success

In 2004, some weeks after the fire, I made the decision to create a PT practice that could run and operate on its own without me. As I was writing down everything that would have to change to accomplish this monumental goal, one thing in particular jumped out at me—numbers.

Prior to the fire, I didn't have a firm understanding of the most important metrics in the practice, nor did I spend any time studying them. As a side note, feel free to substitute terms like key performance indicators, statistics, or numbers for "metrics"—to me, they mean the same thing. I started to investigate and research what the most important metrics to know were and why they mattered. I also wanted to see if there was a way to create a simple "snapshot" of all of the metrics so I didn't have to search all over my EMR and the various spreadsheets we were using.

Whatever is measured improves, and whatever is measured and reported improves dramatically

Soon after my search began, I ran across this great quote from a gentleman by the name of Pearson. It's called **Pearson's**

Law. It states that *whatever is measured improves, and whatever is measured and reported improves dramatically.*

I looked at this principle and surmised that if I don't have metrics, it's impossible to measure the progress of anything. Also, if I'm not aware of which areas to measure, I can't report them.

I began my research with what I thought the important metrics were for each aspect of my business. Later, I studied the metrics other successful practice owners within and outside the physical therapy industry used to understand how their businesses were doing at any given time.

My real struggle was not learning the most important metrics for my practice—it was collecting the data. At the time, most EMR companies weren't overly concerned with creating simple reports that owners could understand and use in their practice. They were more focused on documentation and scheduling. Although reports existed, they had to be printed out in several different areas, and it was extremely difficult to compare numbers.

It took an enormous amount of my time to collect and compile the data and then make sense of it all. I spent nearly every Saturday morning compiling my operational and financial reports.

Of course this process is a little easier with today's advanced EMR systems, but I still believe they miss the mark in creating simple and useful dashboards for owners.

Once I had in place my system for collecting data and sorting it into the appropriate categories, the next step was to make sense of it all. What was good? What was bad? I didn't have any targets with which to compare my data. As I dug down even more by asking others, I realized that there wasn't any consensus of what was "normal." I decided to create my own standard by comparing my current data to my previous data. My starting point was determining what I wanted the end result to be. In simpler terms, I first asked the question, "How much money do I want to make?"

Years later I realized that this is a typical method that successful business people use—starting with the end in mind. By understanding how much money I wanted to make, I knew I could work backwards to determine how many patients I would have to treat, how many new patients I would have to bring into the clinic, how much money I would have to make on average per visit, and so on.

This didn't give me all of the answers, like what my cancellation rate should be, but it helped with many of them. As for the rest of the metrics, I challenged myself (and my staff) to continually beat our previous numbers.

There's a great saying that a mentor of mine shared with me years ago, and I feel it applies just as much now as it did then: *"All progress starts by telling the truth."* I believe this concept came from Alcoholics Anonymous and the 12-Step Program. The first step is admitting you have a problem (i.e., telling the truth).

Telling the truth about my practice wasn't easy. Having numbers glare at me that were not good was a blow to my ego because I knew it was my doing. Prior to this, I would just look at the bank account and if there was money, I felt pretty good about myself and my practice. I can say with conviction that this is an amateur way of running a practice.

What was really invigorating after I gathered the data and interpreted it, was that the *emotion* of the numbers began to dissipate. When I used to think of new patients, collections, and visits, these metrics were mostly not quantified and not managed properly.

However, once I looked at numbers on a spreadsheet, they became nothing more than a non-emotional number. It was as if my brain saw the numbers and, instead of firing up the emotional centers of my brain (i.e., the amygdala), it fired up the problem-solving centers to figure out how to improve the numbers.

Much of my stress and anxiety was related to not knowing

what was really happening in my practice. I was using inaccurate and vague measurements that accentuated my emotion because there wasn't logic and objectivity, only worry and fear.

The result of all of this research led to creating The Simple Financial Dashboard™. This is a tool used to review the most important metrics in the operational and financial areas of a practice. Many owners have modified it to fit their specific practice; however, the principle of using objective measures stands.

There's a saying that my financial advisor used to share back in the day. He said "Jamey, garbage in, garbage out." At the time, the numbers in my practice were garbage. They weren't accurate. Regrettably, I was making important decisions in my practice based on inaccurate data. Of course, the strategies I created were also wrong, leading me to bad results.

My goal was to have a business that didn't rely on me being there 24/7. Unfortunately, I wasn't willing to be completely honest about how my practice was doing. I was lying to myself, preventing my practice from growing. Once I ran across that saying, "All progress starts by telling the truth," I finally got brutally honest with my situation and took full responsibility for the results I was getting. After that, I made sure that every aspect of my practice had metrics supporting the effectiveness of that area. I also made sure that the data was accurate. This led to radical growth in my practice.

One of the biggest reasons I am able to operate my practice remotely (mostly from my kitchen table) is because I have complete awareness and control of every aspect of my business. With accurate metrics, I have the results of each area of the practice at my fingertips, including the front desk, my physical therapists, billing and collections, marketing, and any other area I want to track. This model of tracking and overseeing my practice has given me the greatest freedom and has allowed me to continue to grow the practice without having to be on-site.

There are many metrics one can follow. As long as you put a number to it, you can track it. Below is a list of metrics I use with an explanation of each.

Referrals - number of patients who contact my office.

New Patients - number of patients who come into the office (i.e., evaluations).

Cancellation Percentage - number of visits who are seen compared to the number of visits who should have been seen. At my clinics, we like to see this number below 8%.

Visits - number of patients who are treated and billed.

Visits/New Patients - the number of visits on average a new patient is seen.

Total Capacity - the total number of visits all of your therapists combined can treat in a month.

FTE (Full Time Equivalent) - equal to a full time, 40-hour per week physical therapist (1.0). If you have three PTs working in your clinic and one works 40 hours per week, one works 32 hours a week and one works 20 hours per week, you would have 40 (1.0) + 32 (0.8) + 20 (0.5) = 2.3 FTEs. This number is multiplied by the number of visits 1.0 FTE can treat in a month.

Utilization - how busy (measured by a percentage) the clinic is compared to the total capacity. This is a great way to determine if you are overstaffed, understaffed, or just right. For example, if your total capacity is 100 patients and you are seeing 85, then your Utilization is 85%.

As a side note, I use utilization as the determining factor for how productive the treating clinicians are. I also use these numbers to determine if the time is right to start looking for another PT. My goal is to have my practice running at 85% utilization or higher. I know for a fact that we will be profitable at this number, assuming there are no issues with collections. Once the clinic starts hitting the 95% mark, I analyze the utilization rate against the new patient numbers to determine whether or not the metrics support hiring another PT.

Many times staff will complain about how busy they are. If you don't have objective measures in place, you can get caught up in all of the drama. What I found is that most of the time, it's a time management problem or lack of efficiencies. Only if my utilization is at or above 95% will I consider another clinician.

Workdays - number of treatment days in the month. I like to keep it simple at no more than five days in a week even if we have hours on Saturday. This number is used to determine the total capacity and percent utilization.

Visits/Day - the number of visits the clinic (or therapist) is seeing per day. This lets an owner determine quickly how productive a PT is on a daily basis. Again, many times therapists complain that their schedules are crazy busy; however, I've found that this is a problem with how the front desk person is scheduling patients, NOT how many patients they are treating.

How do you determine how many patients you want your staff to see per day? It really comes down to two things: The first is what it will take for you to be profitable. The second is your personal preference. I expect my PTs to see at least 12 patients per day, or 60 per week. With the help of my bookkeeper, I have determined that we will hit my profitability goals with these numbers based on our current reimbursement amount.

This is less than two patients per hour. In my practice, I don't bonus until 63 visits per week, but I'm only asking them to see a minimum of 60 per week. The reason for this is that I want a little "wiggle" room in case reimbursements change or their billing is a little low for some reason. I want to make sure they receive a bonus out of profits, not out of my own pocket.

Now that we have the raw operations data to run the clinic, it's equally important to understand the basic financials of the practice. Here is my list of financial metrics I look at on a monthly basis with an explanation of each:

Total Expenses - The costs to keep the clinic running. I've been asked many times if I included my salary or draw in this number. Obviously, it will greatly affect one's expenses, especially in a small practice. The answer is I have done both. I have included my salary and draw and other times I excluded my draw. I was confused as to how to do this for many years because I wanted to see my real profitability number. I could skew that number if I took a high salary or draw. The other confusion came from what my accountant wanted me to do from a tax perspective. But this did not give me a clear picture of the monthly operations. Also, I use profitability to pay bonuses for my PTs and directors. If I use up all of the profit as a salary or draw, my staff would get nothing. I finally decided to change a couple of things.

First, my salary (not draw) was solely based on what it would cost for me to replace myself in the practice. When I was treating 40 hours per week, I paid myself equal to the amount it would take to hire another therapist. Second, I had my bookkeeper remove the draw or bonuses I would take from the financial numbers I used to determine bonuses. This was a personal decision. I wanted to see how much profit we were generating so I could pay out bonuses fairly.

I don't believe that there is a right or wrong way for how you do this as long as it works for you. I am not an accountant, so I highly recommend you consult with your accountant. I am just sharing what I did for perspective.

The bottom line is this: be mindful of your expenses.

Cost/Visit (VERY IMPORTANT!) - expenses divided by the number of visits seen. This is a great indicator of profitability. If it costs you too much per visit to deliver care, then you have a few options: increase the number of visits your therapists are seeing, increase the overall amount you're collecting by either coding more efficiently or charging for supplies, and finally, you can lower your costs by cutting expenses. I personally don't like the last option. It's a scarcity mindset. Nobody grows a practice by cutting expenses. You grow a practice by generating more new patients and hiring good people to treat them.

Payroll - I believe payroll should be no more than 1/3 of your total revenue. Of course, this will change depending on the type of practice you have. My practice is an outpatient insurance-based model, so it works for me.

Billed Charges - the total charges you bill a patient for your services.

Billed Charges/Visit - the total amount billed divided by the number of visits seen.

Net Revenue - the total amount of money collected. Most EMR systems will calculate this number, or you can use the amount of money deposited into the bank account. Every month, I have my bookkeeper update this number for me on my financial dashboard. If you have multiple revenue streams, you can always break down this number into net revenue per income source.

Net Revenue/Visit - the amount of money collected divided by the total number of visits seen. As long as this number is higher than expenses/visit, you will be profitable. Many times I see own-ers trying to increase visits to raise this number. However, if it's a low-paying insurance company and it is costing you money to deliver care, it might lower this average instead of increasing it.

Net Revenue/Billed Charge (BC) - the total revenue divided by the amount billed. This one always confuses people, so it is best if I explain it in an example. I charge, on average, around $220 (BC) per visit. The amount of money I collect, on average, is $100 per visit. If I divide $100 by $220, I get approximately 45% of what I bill. Of course, this number will change depending on if you're in-network, out-of-network, or have a cash-based model. I break this down by individual insurance company so

I know exactly my NR/BC per insurance. This helps me make decisions about whether to keep them or not.

If I see this percentage decreasing, I immediately look at my AR (accounts receivable). These numbers are inverse to one another. This tells me to focus more on collections. However, if my AR is relatively unchanged, I'll focus on my payer mix (the mix of different insurance companies we are seeing) or our billing/coding practices.

This percentage helps me (and my staff) identify very quickly where to search for the problem and fix it. Time is money and the longer it takes to collect money from either insurance companies or from patients, the less money will be collected. It is imperative that I have accurate and easy-to-search metrics.

Profit (ALSO VERY IMPORTANT!) – the money remaining after expenses are deducted. RED is bad. BLACK is good. The goal of any practice should be to MAKE MONEY. The only reason your business exists is to generate profit.

Now, I know what you're going to say. "No, I'm here to help my community and to make a difference." Absolutely. However, if you do that effectively, you will also create profit. If you do it poorly, you won't. The value you create in exchange for money determines whether you make money. Just assume that if you're not making any money, you're not providing the value your customers or patients want.

In order to create a profitable business, it is vital to collect, track, and understand your operational and financial metrics.

The truth is harsh, I know, but it's the mindset an owner needs to run a successful practice and help a lot of people.

In order to create a profitable business, it is vital to collect, track, and understand your operational and financial metrics. I have seen many practices improve their bottom line just by tracking their numbers accurately. Don't be overly concerned with figuring out "why" they are down and getting hung up on strategy. Instead, be more concerned with knowing the metrics that are below your targets and sharing them with your staff.

For more information specifically on Chapter 7, Measure for Success, please visit:

www.TheAutomatedProfessionalPractice.com/book/chapter7

CHAPTER 8

How to Troubleshoot Metrics

Now that we have a good understanding of the metrics in our practice, it is time to understand what triggers these metrics to move up or down. Furthermore, we are going to dive deeper into the possible causes and effects of these metrics and quickly determine the potential problems.

If you're able to understand how to use numbers in each area of your practice, it makes it quite simple to keep eyes on your practice anytime you want from anywhere. This is how I'm able to "manage" my practice from my kitchen table or anywhere else there is Wi-Fi.

As an example, let's use the metric of **New Patients**. The first thing I want to know is what is the trend over the past three to six months compared to last year at this time? My next question is what new patient strategies are in place to help increase the new patients.

Not long ago, I wouldn't have been able to answer these questions. Frankly, I had no idea what my marketing strategy was because we didn't have one. I never thought the process of getting new patients into my clinic was a result of "cause and effect." Of course it sounds so simple now, but when you're in the thick of things on a daily basis, it's not so simple.

My thinking was very flawed in the past. I had a non-existent marketing campaign to generate new patients. I was frustrated and confused about why my referrals were dropping. I knew that I must be doing something right because we did have new patients coming in the door. I realized that my challenge was that we were not documenting what we were doing to create these referrals and because of that, we didn't know what to do to repeat the process.

Once I began using the metric of referrals as an indicator of the effectiveness of my marketing, it took the confusion away and marketing for referrals became more of a game. And games are fun.

I decided to focus my energy, creativity, and time on trying to make that referral metric increase. I enlisted the help of my staff to do the same and incentivized them when a referral patient came into the practice. The entire staff became more engaged during the treatments and made it a point to ask patients if they knew someone who was in pain.

In hindsight, using a documented marketing system and tracking metrics to increase my new patient volume is incredibly basic and obvious, but that's the beauty of understanding how to use your metrics. It creates clarity. It simplifies our thinking and helps us focus our time on activities that produce results. It really isn't complicated. What's complicated and frustrating is that most owners don't actually do it.

The next important operational metric is **Cancellation Percentage**. I remember that my cancellation percentage (the number of patients who do not show up for their appointments per week compared to the total number of patients that could have been seen) used to be 16%. That means if 100 patients were scheduled to come in on Monday, only 84 actually came in by close of business Friday. This created a loss of over $1,600 per week in revenue.

Once I began tracking this number and speaking with more successful owners, I found out that the cancellation percentage should be below 10%. I began asking my front desk staff why the cancellations were so high. The problem stemmed from my front desk person not knowing how to handle patient objections.

What's an objection? An objection sounds something like this:

I can't come in today.
I'm stuck at work.
My kids are off school.
I'm having car trouble.

To me, it is a patient saying to us that they have a higher priority than physical therapy: "I have something that is more meaningful to me than coming to physical therapy."

My front desk person usually said something like this, "Oh, okay. No problem. We'll see you next time." This response was costing me tens of thousands of dollars per year.

The solution was easy. I sat down with my front desk person and discussed how to best answer these objections from patients. Of course, the responses wouldn't be 100% effective and reduce our cancellations down to zero. However, my initial goal was to get our cancellations down below 10% and in less than two weeks, it worked.

Again, the solution was so much simpler when I was clear that there was a problem. The cancellation percentage metric was my indicator of whether there was a problem or not. It became a game similar to the new patients metric. Our goal was to do things that lowered our cancellations and avoid actions that increased them.

In addition to training my front desk team, I had another strategy come out of attempting to reduce cancellations. This one had to do with my physical therapists. Once I had metrics being accurately measured, I was able to look more specifically at my individual therapists' cancellation rates. It was evident that some PTs' cancellation rates were lower than others. My rate was the lowest at about 7%.

We began using our deductive reasoning skills to determine the cause. The result came down to communication. More specifically, we discovered that *how* the PT was communicating the plan of care and *what* was being said at the end of each therapy session had a direct bearing on the cancellation rate.

The therapists who consistently communicated to the patients what was going to happen in the next PT session had fewer cancellations. Also, these star therapists asked, after communicating the plan of care during the evaluation:

"Is there anything coming up between now and then, such as work deadlines or a vacation that will interfere with your ability to show up for PT?"

This strategy resulted in significantly fewer cancellations, no-shows, and dropouts.

Give Your Patient a Reason to Come Back.

I determined that it was very costly to assume our patients were going to return for their next visit. Everyone is busy and physical therapy, although important, isn't life or death. As individuals, we are all constantly taking in lots of information and deciding what we're going to do. I thought that if we do not give patients a good reason to show up for the next visit, then something else more important might take its place.

Our motto in the clinic became *Give Your Patient a Reason to Come Back.*

This eventually became a habit with the staff and our cancellations and no-shows dropped from 16% to 6%. This was like getting a $50,000 per year raise.

The simple truth is that we, as physical therapists, must communicate and deliver value each and every time we see a patient. This is increasingly important in today's world of rising co-pays and exploding deductibles. It is also imperative in cash-based practices where 100% of the revenue is provided by patients.

I realize that for some clinicians, these open and honest conversations are uncomfortable. However, if owners really want to reduce cancellations and give themselves a $1,000 per week raise, then they will have to address this communication issue.

If you focus on getting new patients in the door and limiting cancellations, then you're naturally going to increase the number of visits.

What if your visits are dropping, but your cancellation percentage is good? This has happened many times in my practice. This can be tracked by our next metric, Visits per New Patient, or how many patient visits on average a new patient is seen. It has several variables that will affect it.

The first area I look at is Plans of Care. What treatment plan is the therapist suggesting for the patient?

Most of us were not taught in school how to determine a patient's plan of care. Since most states have direct access and a patient doesn't need a doctor's prescription, the plan of care is determined by the untrained therapist. As we speak, research is being done to try to shine light on this subject and provide objective reasoning to determine standards for how many visits it should take to treat various injuries. However, until that happens, your PTs hold the key to patient visits (and your income!) in the palms of their hands.

In my experience, here is why this is a huge problem. Most PTs, without any training, will provide a plan of care that—and listen very closely—will get the least amount of resistance from the patient.

Although treatment is supposed to be all about the patient, we can't help but make it about ourselves. We limit ourselves as therapists. We are constrained by our own fears. The fastest way to overcome these fears is to practice. I, too, used to be very uncomfortable confronting patients when they canceled an appointment, but with practice I'm able to have a conversation with them openly and honestly with their best interests in mind without allowing the emotion of possible rejection creep into my mind.

I discovered the biggest factor that determined the visits per new patient was the PT's previous experience.

History is a great indicator of this metric. I looked at the history of my therapists over previous months and compared their visits per new patient against mine. Obviously, there will be factors that affect this number, for instance, if one therapist treats a lot of Medicare patients with hip replacements versus another therapist who mostly treats acute sports injuries. You can narrow down your focus as much as you want. However, you will still want to track over time how high or low this number is, compared to your target.

I discovered the biggest factor that determined the visits per new patient was the PT's previous experience including the habits they learned either from previous employers or from internships they had during school.

Once I realized just how widely varied our visits per new patients were, I immediately created a training program to help my PTs determine proper plans of care and what constituted the discharge of a patient. This immediately normalized our numbers, creating consistency among therapists.

Since there is no standard of how many visits a patient should have per episode, it's up to owners to decide what the standard is for their clinic. As long as you're comfortable with it, the patients improve, and you get paid for your services, then it is probably fine. Until we get more data to support one particular plan of care per a particular injury versus another, my advice is to create the system that works for you. The next step is to keep an eye on that metric and communicate with the director or individual clinician if it falls below the target.

The next metric is **Capacity** (total number of patient slots). This metric is pretty straightforward. Capacity sets the foundation for one of the most important metrics I track, **Percent Utilization** (percentage of capacity). Percent Utilization helps me determine when to hire another clinical staff member. It answers the questions:

How do you know when to hire someone?

How do you know when to reprimand or fire someone?

The first objective is to have a minimum utilization requirement. This amount, when achieved, should create profit for the company and get at least a 3 to 3.5 return on your salary investment.

For example: If you pay a PT $70,000, then the Percent Utilization should equal $245,000 of revenue generated per year (Salary x 3.5). Next is to divide $245,000 by the average amount of money you collect per visit. Let's say it is $100 for easy math. $245,000/$100 equals 2,450 visits. Divide this by twelve months and you get 204 visits per month. The expectation for the therapist is to treat 204 visits per month or about 51 visits per week.

If you schedule every 30 minutes, then your capacity is 70

per week. That would put your minimum utilization percentage at 73%.

You are now able to create bonuses and other perks based on this percentage.

Let's assume that you are nearing 96% utilization and your referrals are strong. In this case, I would consider hiring another clinician. I can recall several times my staff wanted me to hire someone because they were "crazy busy," but when I looked at this utilization metric it told a completely different story. Trust your numbers.

> ### *My staff is an investment, especially the ones who directly generate revenue*

This metric will also help determine your productive therapists and your non-productive ones. There should be no surprise to anyone if a PT doesn't receive a bonus or doesn't get a raise. They should have access to this number so they know where they stand at all times. Over the years, this has helped me avoid the entitlement attitude that seems to run rampant in our profession.

If this metric is low, look at the PT's cancellation rate, plans of care, and discharge rate. If you're still not sure, ask yourself this question: "Is this person a Superstar?" If the answer is no, then you will have to make a decision as to whether they need more training or somewhere else to work.

The next metric is **Expenses**. This is pretty straightforward. However, it's worth noting that one particular expense should not be viewed as an expense. Several years ago, I had a mindset shift in how I viewed my staff. I used to consider them an expense. In fact, if you ask any CPA, they will tell you that this is exactly how your staff is considered on a profit/loss statement. To me, however, my staff is an investment. Especially the ones who directly generate revenue.

Why does this matter? If you view your staff as an expense and your mindset always says expenses must be cut, then you will always view your staff as something that should be cut instead of appreciated.

Once I began to view my staff as an investment, I wanted to grow that investment, to have it appreciate (like a stock). I changed my approach to nurturing my investment by appreciating my staff. Yes, a little play on words here. But my relationship with them immediately improved and the contentiousness we used to have turned into collaboration.

Watch what happens as you begin to view and treat your staff as investments rather than a cost that needs to be cut.

The next metric is **Revenue** (total amount collected). It's important to understand where your revenue is coming from and who is paying you. It's also important to understand your **Revenue per Visit** (total amount collected divided by the total visits). This allows you to make decisions based on visits, which is much simpler to do.

As a side note, I've tried practically every bonus structure possible in order to boost therapist productivity. Once I became clear on my revenue per visit and the minimum productivity I wanted each PT to have, I began providing bonuses for the number of visits above and beyond their target number.

If the amount you're making per visit is declining, then it is important to know why. It could be insurance companies paying less per code this year compared to last year. At least that's what many of us lay the blame on when our income declines. Actually, there are quite a number of other factors this metric represents. Are you billing appropriately for the services performed? So many times I found my therapists under-billing for services performed. Are you having problems with collections? If so, then your accounts receivable should be increasing. How quickly can you spot an increasing AR?

I remember having a seven figure AR issue just a few years ago. We moved from one EMR company to another and all hell broke loose. It took us almost one full year to rectify the mess and drop our AR to an acceptable range. The saying, "the longer it takes to collect, the less you will collect," rang very true as we only collected about one-tenth of the money owed in AR. That was a huge hit to my cash flow, to say the least.

Another area that can affect your revenue per visit is not collecting co-pays and deductibles at the time of service. This includes not collecting for supplies. Never leave money on the table by failing to max out the billing of your negotiated contracts. If Aetna is only going to pay you $70 per visit regardless of how much you bill, then at the very least bill $70 per visit. Of course you'll perform the services, but again many PTs don't understand this and bill less than what they perform.

If your revenue per visit is greater than your expense per visit (or cost per visit), then you will end up with a **Profit Per Visit** (the profit per visit after expenses).

Next is **Billed Charges,** which is the average amount you bill per visit before insurance reductions. After that is Revenue per Billed Charge (revenue collected divided by amount billed). This is something to keep track of, but because it tends to fluctuate depending on the amount of money billed per session, I don't consider it the most important metric.

The most important metric to track is, of course, **Profit.** Although it is important to turn a profit, this number can be misleading. The total revenue and the expenses will affect profit. Expenses are where our salaries as owners live. You can give yourself a huge raise in the salary and expense department causing a seemingly low profit metric. Likewise, you can do the reverse. I played with this for years. On one hand, my accountant wanted me to take a certain amount of salary versus distribution. On the other hand, I wanted to know how much profit we had without me inflating or deflating the numbers, so that I could accurately pay bonuses to my clinic directors who received a percentage of the profit of their clinic. I don't believe there is one right way to do it, as long as you're clear on the reasons of why you're doing it.

I hope this chapter has opened you up to the idea that metrics are not just a bunch of boring numbers on a spreadsheet, but are a living, breathing report card that constantly gives you feedback as to how your business is doing.

As you can see, making just one change can mean thousands of dollars in your pocket. Nothing I presented in this chapter is difficult. The hardest part is creating new habits, like monitoring metrics while letting go of other non-result-oriented habits.

For more information specifically on Chapter 8, How to Troubleshoot Metrics, please visit:

www.TheAutomatedProfessionalPractice.com/book/chapter8.

PART 3:

THE QUANTUM LEAP

CHAPTER 9

TLC Marketing

In this chapter, I'm going to share with you exactly how I generated word-of-mouth referrals for my practice using a strategy I call TLC marketing. And yes, TLC stands for Tender Loving Care.

During the first two-and-a-half years of running my business, prior to the fire, 95 percent of my patients came to me through internal marketing or "word-of-mouth." I didn't spend one dime on marketing and I was proud of that.

At the time, word-of-mouth marketing was my best and easiest form of patient referrals. My strategy was to grow my practice using word-of-mouth marketing, so I didn't have to buy doctors' lunches.

My thought was that all we had to do was engage deeply with our patients and do everything we could to help them, and then we would grow effortlessly. Boy, was I naive. The biggest mistake was assuming all of my future employees had the same outlook I did on customer service and taking care of people.

As I grew my practice and started hiring, I realized quickly how difficult it was to treat a full schedule of patients while keeping an eye on the staff. I found out that not all physical therapists treated people the way I do. It wasn't so much the technical skills of treating patients that was the issue; it was the lack of attention and focus. I found it amazing that so many PTs had an attitude of "the patient is here for me" instead of "we are here for patients."

The front desk person was worse. Patients started to complain about how rude my front desk person was and that it was very difficult to schedule or ask an insurance question.

Of course, when I asked my front desk person, she had a completely different story and blamed it on the patient. My initial reaction was to support my employee and apologize to the patient. Unfortunately, it happened again and again until I let her go.

I learned the hard way that in order to grow without going insane, I would have to establish a system and standard for customer care, then create a training program to teach all of my employees how to communicate with patients, so we could continue to get word-of-mouth referrals.

Again, I was convinced that if every physical therapist was able generate their own referrals with the support of competent front desk people and good PT aides, then we wouldn't need to spend money on marketing at all.

The remainder of this chapter is how I developed my personal strategies for generating word-of-mouth referrals, and how I created a series of repeatable systems that consistently generates over 60 percent internal referrals per month.

The first lesson I learned in creating word-of-mouth (WOM) referrals is that I was ten times more likely to have a patient refer someone if they were a current patient or client. In other words, they hadn't been discharged and I was seeing them on a regular basis.

The same rule that applies to getting WOM referrals also applies to getting patients to pay co-pays—if you don't collect at the time of their visit, it will not only take considerably longer to collect your money, but the amount collected will be considerably lower. The longer a patient is away from your practice, the less likely they are to refer someone.

Out of Sight, Out of Mind

I believe there are two reasons why I had a waiting list of WOM referrals when I was treating:

1. A great experience
2. I consistently asked for referrals

Most of the therapists who worked for me understood number one. Now, they didn't always know how to do that, but intellectually they understood that a great experience is important.

When it came to reason number two, you would have thought I was asking them to commit a crime. "I can't do that," I heard, or "I'm a PT, not a salesman."

I knew going into this that it wasn't going to be easy, but I honestly felt building an in-house referral marketing system could be done.

I decided to take a step back from everything and take a critical look at what could be improved to help keep patients coming in, even with new staff.

I realized that it started with the front desk person. I feel that the most important person in your company is your front desk person. The front desk person can be the difference between taking home a paycheck or racking up more credit card bills.

A really great front desk person has to be helpful. They have to be caring and able to communicate. They have to know their stuff and connect with patients. When answering phones, they should be clear and pleasant.

My initial approach to organizing the front desk was to leave it up to them. I know. It was stupid of me to think that they would just know what to do, but I didn't have a lot of time to devote to them. I gave them general guidelines like "be friendly," "treat people like you want to be treated," and other meaning-less sayings that were interpreted quite differently from what I anticipated.

It dawned on me that if I was going to create my ideal prac-tice, I actually had to spend a little time thinking about *what* I wanted and *how* I wanted things to be done. Although this may sound simple to some, for me making clear decisions was one of the most difficult things I ever had to do.

How would my perfectionist tendencies ever allow me to make permanent and final decisions the staff could follow?

I would be lying if I didn't tell you that I went through about 20 different ways of answering the phones. After many versions, I finally settled on "Good {morning, afternoon, evening}. Schrier Physical Therapy, this is {NAME}, how can I help you?"

The point of this story is not for you to copy my greeting—it's irrelevant. The take-home message is to spend time deciding what it is you want and to be clear and direct in explaining it to your staff. If you are unclear, then your staff will be unclear, and when your staff is unclear, they will do it their own way, not yours.

Once the greeting was done, I focused on how to schedule a new patient, because that is the most common call we get (at least we hope so).

I began to see firsthand that no two front desk people handled a new patient the same. Although they were using the same EMR system, what they entered and how they entered it was different. This caused a whole host of problems, from reporting being inac-curate to having to decipher coding that wasn't universal.

I could see that we needed to create an entire system for patient intake. I gave my front desk person an overall vision of how I ultimately wanted the front desk to function, the metrics I wanted to achieve and how long I thought it should take to create the system. I left it up to her to develop it. It took some time to get this organized because of front desk turnover, lack of a training system, and switching EMR systems three times. But eventually, an intake process was created.

Our intake process starts at the front desk. Even the most basic of tasks—answering the phone—was inconsistent. Sometimes we answered the phone in one ring and sometimes it was six. Imagine you are in pain and you are calling physical therapy offices. You wait patiently through the first couple of rings, fully expecting the phone to be picked up on the next ring. The call finally picks up and you are put through to a voice mail recording. Would you leave a message, not knowing how soon you'd receive a call back or would you move on to the next name on the list?

In my practice, almost all of our patients have their first experience with us over the phone and I'm sure that's true for your practice as well. You are not guaranteed a new client when you answer the phone but you can certainly lose one if a prospect is sent to voice mail or if the person they first talk to is rude or uncaring. How your office handles incoming calls alone could cause you to lose patients, visits. and thousands of dollars.

Our solution was to create a phone policy. We would answer the phone by the third ring no matter what. Our old phone system necessitated asking someone to cover the phones if the front desk person had to step away. This challenge led us to upgrade our phone system, allowing us to forward calls automatically and ensuring that the phones were always covered.

The phone policy included a standard script for answering the phone as well as basic phone etiquette. Poor phone manners are a direct reflection on the professionalism of your business and a sure turnoff to prospective patients as well as current clients.

What really separates a good front desk experience from a bad one is how questions and objections are handled. Whether it's a simple question about scheduling appointments or something more personal like money, objections allow your staff to shine or perish!

An objection could be a question of why we collect co-pays at the time of service or why we schedule out the full plan of care. They are usually questions, concerns, or things that are unclear to a patient. One of the most common issues we had involved communicating insurance benefits to patients. Our front desk people were not clear in their explanation of a person's benefits. This caused a decrease in trust and many times, a loss of patients. Without clarity, you're guaranteed to create a less than positive experience for your patients. This will ultimately have a negative effect on your bank account.

Most objections from patients stem from either a preconceived idea or a previous experience that they need more clarity on. Many times the front desk person views this as a challenge or threat to them. This creates an unnecessarily unpleasant experience for both the patient and the staff member. Once we realized that most objections are really a communication issue, we created scripts that succinctly yet fully answered people's questions.

The first step was to have my front desk person write down every single objection and question she received. Taking it one step further, I also asked patients about their experiences directly: "What do you think of physical therapy? What are some of the frustrations you have when you go to physical therapy or chiropractic or any doctor's office?" I shared the results with my front desk person and the rest of the staff.

For me, the best part of this entire process of understanding objections was sitting down and formulating how to respond to them. It forced me to really think about how I wanted to operate my practice and what I wanted my clients' experience to be. It was a little time-intensive on my part, but much less costly than answering patients' questions incorrectly or with the wrong tone and upsetting them. (Plus, I only had to do it once!) I was relentless in asking myself, "How would I want someone to answer me?" Whether it was how to address communicating insurance benefits or how to greet someone walking into the office, the answers were written down, the staff knew how to respond, and patients received calm and consistent answers to their objections. Best of all, their objections helped ME gain clarity on my practice!

In addition, many times I didn't know the answer, so I asked the staff for help. They became a big part of solving these issues. This helped create more buy-in from my staff, which increased their overall experience as an employee.

Here's an example of how we handled the issue of when and how to explain insurance benefits. We ended up incorporating this into our intake process. The results were huge.

"So, Ms. Smith, what I'd like to do right now, if you have a few more minutes, is to verify your insurance benefits. Once your benefits are verified, we will give you a call and tell you exactly what your benefits are, and answer any questions you may have prior to coming in for your initial evaluation. Would that be okay? What's the best number and time to reach you?"

> **This simple communication tells the patient so much more than just their benefits. It tells them about WHO WE ARE.**

I can't tell you how much money I have made because of this simple communication; it's in the tens of thousands or even hundreds of thousands of dollars. The reason is this simple communication tells the patient so much more than just their benefits. It tells them about WHO WE ARE.

They know that we are not in the business of using bait and switch or other nefarious tactics to get them into the office and then surprising them with how much they owe for the visit.

Instead, their trust level shoots up, creating an immediate good vibe on the very first call, even before they come in.

In this case, we handled the issue of insurance verification right from the beginning. It's an example of how you can pre-empt an objection before the patient has to ask. The more you do that, the more trust and confidence you will build with your patients. This will no doubt lead to more patients, referrals, and money.

Here is another example of handling a common question/objection from a prospective patient: *"Will I just be doing exercise in physical therapy?"*

This one used to make my blood boil. The way I answer that question is by replying with a question to understand further why they think that way about PT.

Let's assume a prospect's problem is back pain.

Prospect: *"So Jamey, will physical therapy help my problem or will I just be doing a bunch of exercises?"*

Me: *"What makes you ask that?"*

Prospect: *"I don't know. I've just heard that from people."*

Me: *"Cool. Well, I'm not sure if or how I can help you. Let me find out a bit more about your situation, and then I'll have a better idea of what we can do for you."*

Prospect: *"Sure, that would be great."*

I proceed with my subjective assessment and ask them questions like, "What happened? How long have you had pain? Does it radiate?" This can be done with both prospective and new patients who are not sure if physical therapy is right for them.

When you are trained how to answer any objection a prospect may have, you are empowered to convert prospects to patients and you can teach your staff to do the same.

This method allows me to really understand the other person's thinking and how to address the real problem they have.

More often than not, the real question they are asking is *"Jamey, can you help me?"*

My time is extremely valuable and I treat it as such. I don't invest my time with people who are not serious about getting the results they want. I realize that when people ask me things in a "challenging" manner, it is really not a challenge. What they really want to know is *"Jamey, can you help me?"*

Remember, if we perceive a challenge or objection from a person as a threat, we will respond very differently than if we perceive it as a need for help and a desire for greater understanding. You will generate much more business using the latter.

Appointment Reminders

Another simple strategy to help increase patient show-up rates is to send out appointment reminders. If you are using an EMR system, most will have this feature. My recommendation is to use it.

People nowadays are busier than ever. Whether it's spending hours on social media, working on our laptops, or participating in family activities, people's lives are full and it is commonplace to forget appointments. Fortunately, it is easy to create a process to remind people of their appointment. You can use email, calls, or texting. I like to have things as automated as possible to reduce the number of times I have to ask the front desk person to stop what they're doing to make reminder calls

Automated emails are very common, but reminder texts are becoming more popular because people are more likely to read a text than an email.

Whatever method is the easiest and most likely for you to do consistently should be the one you use. A system only works if you use it.

The other thing I do along the lines of appointment reminders is let the patient know what to expect on their next visit. This is something that I thought everyone did. It just makes so much sense to let your patients know what they can expect in their next appointment.

Of course, I'm communicating ahead of time in order to head off a possible question or uncertainty. It's amazing how many times I hear from people about how they don't have a clue about what they're doing in PT. Trust me when I tell you uneducated patients have a hard time referring others to PT.

Here is an example of what I say:

Me: "Ms. Smith, when is your next appointment?"

Patient: *"Oh, I think it's next week."*

Me: "Let's check on that to make sure."

In some cases, the patient knows when their next appointment is… "It's Thursday, 8 a.m." This is usually a patient who is on board and committed to getting better. Those two subtle differences are huge, and confirming the next appointment is paramount. I'm asking the question to reinforce the importance of coming to the next appointment. People are busy. If they can take something off their list (i.e., a PT session), they will. It's up to the therapist, aides, and front desk person to reinforce the importance of showing up.

Your patient is one visit away from not showing up anymore.

Me: "Ms. Smith, your appointment is Thursday at 10 a.m. We're going to focus on really stretching your back out so you can get moving better, because I know you're feeling really stiff, all right? Make sure you're here on time so we can get started right away."

Patient: *"Sounds good. Thank you."*

Always give them a reason to come back.

This seemingly inconsequential communication does three things:

1. It confirms their appointment time.
2. It gives them a compelling reason to not skip their appointment.
3. It reinforces that you are in charge and know what you're doing.

Remember, you're competing with other appointments and activities that the patient could be doing.

Physical Therapy isn't heart surgery. Most patients have the attitude that they can skip their appointment and it won't affect the outcome. Never assume that just because you discussed a plan of care a few weeks ago, it's enough. Remind them on every appointment.

The Patient Experience

Be on time! Patients do not like waiting—none of us do. Create a process to avoid having the patient wait. They will appreciate it.

I also recommend creating a process for therapists or aides to introduce themselves to people.

This may sound obvious, but there's a big difference in saying, "Hello, I'll be working with you today," and "Hello, Ms. Smith. My name is Jamey Schrier, your physical therapist, and I'm looking forward to working with you today."

Here are a few mindset things I do prior to introducing myself that motivate me:

- Get excited – you don't have to be over the top, but acting like you're happy to be working with someone is better than having them feel like you could care less.
- Think to yourself—this person fuels my livelihood and my children's future.
- This person is worth $3,500. Why $3,500? That's the lifetime value of this person. I average $1,000 in collected revenue on every new patient. If they come back to me for PT over the course of their lifetime, it may add up to three or four times, or $3,000 to $4,000. And that doesn't include any referrals I might receive.

Introduce yourself with that in mind. Treat them as a $4,000 investment. Don't take them for granted. Treat every single person this way whether they're coming in one time or 25. Every person who comes into your office is helping you get closer to what you want. They are giving opportunities to your staff. They are helping your family. This is the mindset that I have as I greet every single person.

These are the secrets that helped me create a two to three week waiting list, all by word-of-mouth referrals, when I first started. These are the things I know work. This is the mindset that my staff operates from, and it's working for them just as well, if not better than it worked for me.

The Evaluation

We're going to get into how to do an evaluation. This isn't school, so I'm not going to teach you how to do an evaluation from an academic standpoint, because you already know how to do that. What I'm going to teach you is how to do an evaluation from a referral standpoint.

The first part of the evaluation is the **Subjective**. We all know that, right? Subjective is all about asking questions and gathering insight. So you want to ask questions with an *interested* mindset versus an *interesting* mindset. What's the difference, you ask?

Being interested in your patients is about intent listening and engagement. You are asking questions to learn more and understand more. Conversely, being interesting is about having the focus on you rather than the patient. A clown in a circus is interesting because the focus is on the clown. It's all about the clown. As a professional health care provider and marketing expert, you want the focus on your patients as much as possible. When given a chance, people love to talk about themselves, and when it comes to other people's pain, most don't want to listen. Their spouse is tired of hearing about it and so are the kids and neighbors. You are giving them the space to do that while directing the conversation.

Now, there is one caveat to what I just said. Since you are in control, make sure that you ask questions to elicit the information you want and need. All of us have come across patients who will talk our ears off. We are running a business, so it's important to tailor your questions. Make sure you have good eye contact, be genuine, be pleasant, be engaging, and don't forget to smile.

This type of Subjective questioning will create a deeper connection with your patients and reward you for years to come.

I'm not going to spend a lot of time on the **Objective** evaluation because all of us should know how to do this. The only advice I would give is to communicate what you're doing. I don't go into the "why" so much, because that tends to spark questions that I'd much rather answer in the assessment portion of the evaluation.

During the **Assessment** part, when I'm explaining what I have found, I really like using diagrams, pictures, or models. Visual aids augment my explanation and create a more concrete understanding in the patient. It also helps me stay focused and on track. I avoid using a lot of medical jargon unless there's a picture to support it or if I'm treating a medical professional.

During the Assessment, it's your time to shine. It's time to be interesting. Here's my method of how I do the Assessment:

- Explain what you found in the Subjective and Objective evaluations and why it is important or not important.
- What they should do.

For example, here is how I link everything together:

"Based on the repetitive work you described to me that you have been doing, sitting at the computer for the past several years, and what I found during the exam with your inability to turn your neck, it appears you have a stuck vertebrae and muscle spasms known as trigger points in this area of your spine. This is causing your inability to move the way you want and eliciting pain."

"So here's what we're going to do, Ms. Johnson. What we're going to..." And then just lay out your approach clearly.

I imagine if you are a business owner, you are good at this part of the evaluation. However, this is more about how your staff PTs perform an evaluation, not you. Look at this section from a perspective of teaching them how to do it the right way—your way.

Again, use pictures, books, models, and posters they can attach meaning to.

"I recommend first working on your posture. You see this person right here, you see their posture?"

Use an iPad app to help explain. They're fantastic. There are so many different kinds of apps that show the body. So grab an iPad, put one of these anatomical apps on it, and you could sit there with your iPad and show them what's going on.

"Here's what's going on with you, here's what we're going to do, and here's the approach we're going to take."

Again, go deep in explaining, educating, and showing them what is happening. This will be extremely important to set the stage for family and friend referrals later on.

Now for the final part of our *SOAP* evaluation – the **Plan**. This is what I call my million-dollar question, because I've built my million-dollar practice with this question. After you've explained what you're going to do and why, it's time for the how. Here is an example:

Me: *"Okay, Ms. Johnson, I explained what I think is going on with your back and what I can do to help you. Do you have any questions so far?"*

Patient: *"No."*

Me: *"Great. Based on what you have and my experience working with this problem, it will take 12 sessions to hopefully fix it I would like to see you three times a week for four weeks Initially, we'll focus on eliminating your pain and improving your motion. Then we'll focus on strengthening and stabilizing the area and getting you back to tennis. Do you have any questions?"*

If they have questions, address them right then and there. Once you've answered all of their questions, ask the Million-Dollar question:

Me: **"Is there anything coming up in the next four weeks, either work-related or vacations, that will affect your ability to commit to the plan of care?"**

Don't say a word. Let it sink in. Give them a minute to think about it if need be.

Why is the question so important? You're asking for an agreement. You're asking them for a commitment of time and money in exchange for good health.

Patient: *"No, I should be pretty good."*

Me: *"Great, because when you leave today I want you to schedule all of your visits at the front desk to reserve the time and day that works best for you."*

This simple strategy will immediately fill in empty slots because they're scheduling out all of their visits, reduce your cancellation rate due to an increase in their commitment, and increase referrals due to their positive experience.

It will also increase patients' commitment to their health.

Finally, I ask them if they're ready to get started. I introduce them to the team, including my PT aides, and let them know they will be working with them as well as me, but not to worry; I'm in full control of everything that they're doing.

I get the patient's commitment first to schedule the appointments. Next, I handle any objections that they may have right then and there, and then I start treatment. I realize that other people have different ways of doing it. If it is working for you, then I wouldn't change a thing.

However, there is one thing that many therapists are being taught in school that I disagree with. PTs are being told that if you find something wrong with the patient, go ahead and treat the problem immediately. I don't agree with this approach. Oh, and by the way, I used to do it.

Just as I wouldn't expect a surgeon to say, "Jamey, you're having trouble breathing? I'll go ahead and cut you open and take a look at it," I don't treat first. No. Let's get all the facts we need first, create an assessment and plan, and then begin treatment. This way you can explain everything to the patient step-by-step in an orderly fashion, handle any questions they have, and get a commitment to care.

When I used to treat on the run, I wasn't nearly as successful, productive, or efficient with the patient. I didn't get anywhere near the same level of commitment from them and I received fewer referrals. After asking patients which approach they liked better, they unanimously chose the organized one because it had continuity.

Patients want to understand what is going on, the reasoning behind what I'm doing, and the plan. They're not expecting you to treat them five minutes after showing up to their appointment. This feedback caused me to change my approach.

Another communication tip is to ask during each treatment session, "How are you doing? How was the last session?" I know it sounds simple, and many of us do this already, but remembering to *actually listen* to their answers is the secret.

Sometimes I would even ask them to rate their previous session: "All right, so how would you rate your last session?" This isn't anything scientific. It's just a way for me to sense how they feel PT is going and whether they have any concerns. If they gave the PT session a low score, like a four out of ten, it gives me an opportunity to find out exactly why it was low and address the problems immediately.

Quality Assurance Forms. The number one strategy that has helped me generate numerous referrals is the QA (Quality Assurance) form. Usually on the fourth or fifth session, (about two weeks into therapy) I have the patient fill out a simple, one page questionnaire.

The reason I do this within two weeks is because this is the time patients will start to make the decision on whether physical therapy is working or if they like the care they are getting. If people are going to cancel, it usually happens more frequently after a few PT sessions.

The QA form questions include:

- How are you feeling since you started PT?
- What percentage improvement do you feel you've made since starting PT?
- Have you had any difficulties scheduling?
- Would you come back to Schrier PT?

- Do you feel comfortable enough to refer a family member or friend, and if so, do you know somebody who could benefit from seeing me?"

This last question is asked if, and only if, the patient is doing well and is happy with their experience thus far. Patient first. Then referral.

When a patient is feeling better, it is normal for them to feel appreciative, and many times they want to show their appreciation. If you do not tell them what you want (i.e., recommend a family member or friend to me), they will choose their own way to say "thank you." This is why we get so much food at our clinics. I would much rather have a referral than bagels.

Remember, QA forms can be used any time you want. I often use them for re-evaluations or as a follow-up to a technique I was trying. I can't tell you how many times doing this has kept a patient from canceling. They say "You know, Jamey, I'm really glad we had this talk because I wasn't sure if I was going to stay with physical therapy." This simple form has been directly responsible for bringing in tens of thousands of dollars of potentially lost revenue due to patient cancellations and drop-outs.

Re-evaluations are really just the same process as the initial evaluation. Ask your questions, go through your objective part, go through your assessment, and then go through your plan.

Here's a beautiful part about the re-evaluation: There are only four possible outcomes from a re-evaluation:

1. Discharge: they achieved their goals.
2. Continue physical therapy: need more time but on the right track.
3. Continue physical therapy: need to change treatment approach.
4. Refer out: PT isn't working.

By the way, one of the best ways to get tons of referrals from doctors is by referring patients to them. Doctors, like us, love referrals. There's no better way to build a relationship with a doctor than by referring him or her patients first. I promise that they will reward you many times over for every patient you refer.

I've had many doctors tell me "Jamey, you're the only physical therapist who refers patients to me. Most just want me to refer to them." I encourage my staff to refer a patient out to a doctor if he or she is not improving or if they want a doctor's perspective. It's amazing how doctors often do this with each other, but PTs rarely refer anyone out.

Another thing I do to make it easy to refer to me is offer free screenings if a person is somewhat hesitant about physical therapy. I offer to speak with them on the phone first or by email.

One of the best things I have done to keep my practice busy is to follow up with patients via emails and handwritten notes. Every new patient receives a handwritten note saying:

"Dear John,

"Thank you for choosing Schrier Physical Therapy. I'm really looking forward to working with you on your (fill in the blank) and helping you (fill in the blank on why they're here). Please let me know if there's anything I can do.

"Best, Jamey"

This was so well-received by patients and it is standard operating procedure for me and all of my PTs.

If you're not a writer, try sending them a short email. The bottom line is to engage and connect with your patients. Yes, it's a little time consuming, but often your support staff can help. Either way, I have found that it is NEVER a waste of time.

I like to make a big deal over discharges. When there's an agreement between you and the patient and they've achieved their goals, or at least maximized their progress, to me, it's time for a celebration. It is also a good time to ask for testimonials and success stories. Again, they want to thank you. If you ask for a testimonial, there's a good chance they'll be happy to give it to you right then.

I hope you have a gotten a few ideas or strategies that you can add to your existing marketing campaign to generate many more patients.

Remember: There are many more people who need your services than there are people to provide it to them.

Make it easy for people to refer to you.

For more information specifically on Chapter 9, TLC Marketing, please visit:

www.TheAutomatedProfessionalPractice.com/book/chapter9.

CHAPTER 10

Live Event Marketing

In this chapter, we're going to cover how to generate new patients through live events. And when I say events, it could also mean seminars you have, either in or outside of your practice, or even health fairs.

The results I have created by doing live events over the years have generated tens of thousands, if not, hundreds of thousands of dollars and brought many new patients into my two clinic locations over the last 10 years.

One of our best live event sources for new patients is local races. My staff and I loved working with runners, but at first, I was a bit stuck on where to find them. A little research revealed that there were a ton of races close to my clinics. There seemed to be races every weekend. So, I created a referral-generating process via running events.

Prior to this event strategy, I could barely get anyone coming in to the clinic. I relied on the middle man doctor to refer them to me. It was passive marketing at its worst: sitting, waiting, and hoping patients would come and feeling powerless in the process.

The event marketing system changed all that. This income stream alone is responsible for well over $100,000 in revenue over the last several years in my practice, and much more to other owners I've shared this strategy with. Most importantly, it puts the practice owner in control of generating prospects.

When I first started doing running events, I was the person at the event doing the screenings and engaging with the participants. However, my goal was always to delegate this activity to my staff PTs who had an interest in working with runners. Three years after my first event, I have completely created a consistent referral-generating process that doesn't rely solely on my efforts or giving up my weekends with my family.

Can you imagine that? Having a system that is completely in your control to consistently generate new patients any time you wanted? What's best about creating this initial process was that we continually improved it. After every event we looked at what worked well and what needed tweaking. Our results continued to improve and new patients continued to flow in, week after week.

Below is my step-by-step process of exactly what I did to build this six-figure new patient referral process. If you already have an existing system of doing events that works for you, perfect. Maybe you can grab a couple of nuggets and add them to your existing process. If you don't have any system in place, then feel free to follow my process.

If you don't treat runners, then no worries. Use the framework and tailor it to your ideal patient population. Use what works for you.

The Running Event Strategy

Step One: Who is your tribe?

I love that word "tribe." It's a term to describe your group, your audience, and the people with whom you wish to build your company. Define your target audience. Who do you want your future raving fans to be? What type of patients do you love to treat?

Here's a little story about how *not* choosing your target

audience can affect your practice and life. When I first opened my doors in 2001, I loved treating and was good at it. I invested a lot of money and time learning how to be the best. My unique talent was incorporating manual therapy techniques into my treatment style.

My reputation spread quickly and in only a few months, I had a waiting list. It doesn't sound like a problem, right? However, over time, the patients I liked to treat (orthopedics and athletes) became fewer and fewer and my practice was inundated with the chronic pain population. This is a physically and emotionally taxing population to treat.

My intention of treating an athletic population was not congruent with my actions of attracting an athletic population. Instead, I accepted anybody who came in the door and was happy to be busy. If I had to do it over again, I would have focused on the audience I really wanted to treat and incorporated marketing strategies to attract them to my practice from the start.

The take-home message of this story is to focus on a specific audience or tribe and align all of your marketing efforts to attract them to your practice. It may sound counter-intuitive not to branch out widely, but trust me, you will still get patients coming to your practice who are outside of your target audience. However, you will have a better balance of your ideal patients and the non-ideal patients.

Step Two: Book the Calendar

It's time to schedule the events on your calendar. Start the process of booking events with your target population. If your target population is Medicare, focus on giving talks surrounding fall and balance prevention at the YMCA or active retirement communities. The goal is to get into motion with your project.

I recommend scheduling at least six events over the next three months. That's two events per month. This should be enough activity to get a few new patients in the door as well as to create momentum to build on. The goal here is to build momentum and generate a buzz for the program you're offering. Many times a strategy fails not because it wasn't a good idea, but because it doesn't gain enough traction and momentum to take off.

The hardest part of the event strategy is getting it going. Once you have it rolling, it is easy to continue the momentum and improve the process. Make a conscious 90-day effort and get going.

One tip I learned is that the closer the event is to your office, the more patients will come. If you're doing an event that's five miles away and you live in New York City, I doubt your prospects will travel to PT. I have done events that were an hour away, like the Marine Corps Marathon which had 26,000 runners, and got only a couple of new patients. I've also done events two miles away with 200 runners and had 10 people to come in. Proximity helps. My advice is to measure everything and compare your results versus your costs. Let the numbers decide whether you do the event again.

Step Three: Staff It the Right Way

As I mentioned before, when I first started I was the physical therapist who engaged with the runners and gave some basic advice. However, my intention was to make this process automated so I would not always be the person on site. Initially, you may want to be the person on site just to experience it yourself. Once you have your system set up, you will want to get your other PT staff involved.

I have never met an owner who had a problem keeping their schedule full. It's the staff clinicians whose schedules are porous. The therapist who is engaging with the public at the event will also be the therapist those patients will want to see. Involve your

PTs as soon as possible, even if you are there in an overseeing capacity.

I recommend having a minimum of two people at each event:

1. **The Host**

   The host is the person who sets up the entire event. This can be your marketing person or an aide. Their job is to manage the project, from set-up to follow-up. The host is organized. They have great follow-through traits and are someone you can count on. They have a pleasant, friendly, and engaging personality.

2. **Physical Therapist**

   The other person attending the event is the PT. Although every PT should have an opportunity to do the events, I would start with a therapist who has an engaging personality and who also wants to work with the population you're targeting. The PT who brings in the most internal referrals is usually the person who will be successful at events. However, ultimately the PT who is most successful at events is the one who generates the greatest number of prospects and this may not be your PT with the office track record. You may be pleasantly surprised.

Another tip is to have a PT and/or host who can speak the lingo of the population. If you're working with the golf population, it's important to understand the difference between a birdie and a bogey, and a driver versus a wedge. Otherwise, your credibility could be questioned.

Step Four: Proper Set-Up

1. **Six-foot table** – Usually provided at running events.
2. **Tablecloth** – You can go with the cheap plastic cover, however, I recommend a nice tablecloth with your logo on it. A dark tablecloth with a bright logo is best. It stays clean and is very visible.
3. **Signage** – We use an eight-foot standing sign. It is very visible from a distance and allows us to communicate with our audience.
4. **Informational Materials** – Brochures, business cards, and any other material that is relevant to your audience.
5. **Giveaways** – Candy, pens, stress balls, stickers, etc. I wouldn't recommend spending a lot of money on give-aways. I have found zero correlation between expensive giveaways and an increase in referrals.
6. **Screening Area** – Use a portable massage table and a chair. Also, be sure to have cleaning wipes to use after each person is screened. DON'T use table paper. I tried it and it was a disaster.
7. **Exercise Area (optional)** – At some events we created a small "treatment" area consisting of exercise balls, foam rollers, stretch bands, and other supplies used with runners. Recently, we've gotten away from doing this and our results have actually improved. Give it a try and decide for yourself.
8. **Intake Sheet** – You can use paper (like I used to) or an iPad as long as you get the prospect's information. Make sure you write down their name, cell phone number, email address, injury/complaint, and what they want help with. Also have an open section for the therapist to write in recommendations.

Step Five: Engaging the Prospect

Use simple engagement questions to begin a conversation with your prospect.

"How was your run?"

"Did you run as well as you hoped to?"

"Did you have any pain or discomfort that slowed you down?"

Does it matter if they say yes or no? Not really.

For example, you say, "How was your run today? Did you have any pain or discomfort while running?" If they say no, my response is, "That's great. Do you have any goals in the near future of increasing your distance or beating your personal best?"

These are questions to get them thinking of what they want and because you asked the question, the assumption is that you can help.

If they answer yes, then ask them this: "Would you like me to take a look to possibly shed some light on the problem? It'll only take a minute and there's no charge for this." The next step is to pass them onto the host to fill out the intake form. After that, ask your questions and perform your screening.

Once you have enough information to make a recommendation, it's time for you to shine. Tell the prospect what you think. Give them direction on to how to fix this problem. It could be a referral to a doctor or to come in to your clinic for a more thorough evaluation. Be genuine and focus on what will help them.

> *Tip: I have received many referrals by actually referring the prospect to a doctor first for an X-ray or more information. It's a win-win-win situation: Patient – Doctor – You.*

Step Six: The Simple Assessment

Keep your assessment simple and easy to understand. Do not use all of the anatomy language that you learned in school. Do not be complicated. I know it sounds obvious, but I can't tell you how many times my therapists explained what they thought was going on as if they were speaking to another medical professional. Simplicity is best.

Step Seven: The Perfect Solution

Everyone you speak to will want one thing: direction. They want to know what they should do now and whom they should see. An astute physical therapist who is genuine will give them that direction. As I mentioned earlier, the direction may not be to go to your office—it may be to go to a doctor. Your primary duty is to provide direction that will benefit the prospect first and foremost.

What if physical therapy is appropriate? Now what? Explain what they need to do in order to come in and see you. Explain what they can expect from you. Handle any questions or objections they may have. The more clarity they have as to what you will do and what to expect, the better chance they will follow through and become a patient or client.

The last thing I do is give them a few tips they can try before coming into my office. It could be a simple stretch or to use ice or heat. I'm just providing a little extra value to show the person how we do things at Schrier PT. I also would give them my email address and invite them to email me with any questions. Ninety-five percent of the time they don't email, but I've received feedback that it was nice that I offered.

The final thing you want to do is communicate to the host a summary of the interaction with the prospect. It's much easier to tell them what you recommended than to try to take notes yourself. It ensures that you can recall all of the recommendations you made and also helps keep you efficient during the event.

Step Eight: The Foolproof Follow-Up

Nothing is more important in determining your success than the follow-up. No matter how great you are at the event engaging with prospects, if you do not follow up with them, then the number of people actually showing up at your office will plummet.

The secret to following up is to schedule out time to do it. In addition, you want to have a follow-up strategy for each person you spoke to whose information you obtained. How do you follow up? Whether you're calling to confirm their office appointment or calling them to see how they are doing since the race, it's vital to reach out to them.

If you spoke with the person or did some type of screen, the call or email will center around how they are doing and if they have had a chance to do the exercises you suggested.

If they are not on the schedule and are interested in coming in, book the appointment right then. DO NOT WAIT. Hand them over to your front desk person.

What if they're not interested in scheduling? In this case, try to help them by giving them advice or something to do on their own. Here's an example of a follow-up conversation:

Me: "Hi, Mrs. Smith. It was great meeting you at the event last Saturday. I just wanted to see if you had any questions about what we talked about and whether or not you wanted to schedule. I have a time open tomorrow."

Mrs. Smith: *"Hey, thanks, Jamey. I appreciate it. I'm still doing the stretches. I really don't have time in the next couple weeks to come in, but thank you so much. I'll let you know."*

Me: "Is there anything I can do at least in the meantime to help you out? Maybe give you another stretch or something?"

Mrs. Smith: *"Actually, that would be great. Do you have something?"*

Me: "Sure, I have something. I can go ahead and email you a stretch that I want you to do."

Now Mrs. Smith feels good about our relationship and it gives me an opportunity to follow up with her again and to give her other tips in future emails or newsletters.

Step Nine: The Event Success Audit

The event is over. Follow-up calls and emails have been made. You have new patients scheduled. Now what? Next to following up, this might be the most important aspect of the entire event strategy: the audit.

It's time to reflect on the entire event. There has been nothing more critical for improving the event process and my success than this step. We can always improve, make the process a little better or a little easier, or a little less confusing.

On a piece of paper write down:

- What worked well?
- What could you do differently to improve the process?
- What is the next action step?

We did a running event that had 2,500 people attend. We only had one PT on site and she was crushed because of the number of people wanting to talk to her. We learned from it. The next year we had three therapists on site and we tripled the number of new patients. This simple audit exercise was responsible for $15,000 in additional revenue.

You can also go a little bit further with the audit process. Ask yourself how you can use technology to make things better. As I mentioned before, we initially did our intake form on paper. Later on, we upgraded to iPads for increased legibility and ease of use. It's all about using your experience as learning tools to improve your systems and results.

For more information specifically on Chapter 10, Live Event Marketing, please visit:

www.TheAutomatedProfessionalPractice.com/book/chapter10.

CHAPTER 11

Digital Age Marketing

One of the largest factors that helped me take my business to the next level was leveraging technology. Technology allows us to do things better, faster, cheaper, and more easily than ever before. It provides the power we need to scale our practices. As you read this chapter, continue to ask yourself how to use technology to leverage your time, efforts, and energy to create exponential results. The use of technology in your practice, more than any other suggestion in this book, will create some of the most rapid, positive results.

The first technological advance I incorporated was a website. Yes, I know, it sounds a little obvious, but a website, when used correctly, can be a powerful marketing tool that allows me to connect with people WITHOUT taking my time. This was the first time I realized how technology really could help me achieve my goal of an automated practice.

Below are a few technology strategies I used to generate leads, prospects and new patients, as well as streamline systems and processes.

Strategy One: Collecting Leads

Continuing to attract people to your practice is paramount to the vitality and success of your practice. A lead is nothing more than basic information from someone who is interested in your services. An easy way to capture leads is through your website.

The problem that many practice owners have is that they think the website is only for *giving* information to possible prospects. However, the real reason to have a website is to engage with people visiting your site. The easiest way to engage with a lead is to give them something of value in return for their name and email address.

The marketing term for this is "ethical bribe." It allows you to get a person's email with their permission, in exchange for a valuable piece of content. Here are a few content ideas I've used:

- E-books
- Newsletters
- Helpful Exercises or Tips
- Memberships
- Coupons
- Free Screenings

You may be thinking "But Jamey, can't you just give me the thing that works the best?" Everyone's practice and audience are different. The best method is whatever generates the most leads for you. You will need to try several different giveaways, and measure the results to see what works best for you.

The best part of this strategy is that you can do it for free. For example, let's say you offered "Three Simple Exercises to Eliminate Mild Back Pain." As physical therapists, we could easily create a video or write down three home exercises in a matter of minutes. The knowledge we have is vast AND very valuable for people with mild back pain. All we would have to do is shoot a quick video with our smart phone and create an easy way for people to access it. That's it.

The ethical bribe's job is to share your knowledge with people searching for answers to their problems in exchange for their email address. This is still the number one method for collecting leads on the Internet and it's amazingly simple, powerful, and—don't forget—free!

This process of capturing the email address of someone who just downloaded your "Simple Exercise" video, who is interested in help for their mild back pain, is called generating a lead. Your video is constantly searching for leads 24/7. Imagine how much time it would take to talk to 20 people about their back pain symptoms. With this strategy, you could get 20 leads in 15 minutes. The Internet never gets tired and never closes.

Now what?

It is time to turn your lead into a prospect. We generate many leads every month. However, if they don't end up as a patient in our clinic, we don't actually make any money. A prospect, unlike a lead, has a stronger interest in what your services can do for them. If someone opts-in to receive your "Simple Exercises" video, that's a lead. If that same person ends up coming into your clinic for a free screening, that's a prospect. The person has a stronger interest in your services and makes a stronger commitment. In this case, the person is committing their time.

Obviously, the next step is to convert them into a new patient.

Lead ⇨ Prospect ⇨ New Patient

Almost 20% of our patients come into our clinic using this one strategy. This equates to hundreds of thousands of dollars every year with a marketing cost of virtually nothing.

The secret to an effective lead strategy campaign using your website is to have an easy way for the person to enter their name and email. The easiest way to do this is to ask your website designer to create an opt-in form. I recommend that this is placed on the upper portion of the visible screen and on every page. If you need to hire someone to do this, I recommend websites like Upwork.com or Fiverr.com.

Strategy Two: Direct Response Marketing

In order to win, it's imperative to keep score. Unfortunately, it's something that I never did. When people would ask me how I was doing, my response was the typical "I think I'm doing pretty well." The reality was that I had no idea how I was doing because I wasn't measuring or keeping track of anything.

Remember **Pearson's Law**: *"That which is measured improves. That which is measured and reported improves dramatically."*

Keeping score is a way to use Pearson's Law and measure progress. For a long time my marketing efforts were not measured and I could only guess at their effectiveness. However, once I learned Pearson's Law, I looked for marketing strategies that I could specifically measure to know for sure whether they were effective or not.

One of the marketing strategies I discovered is called direct response marketing. Simply put, it's a marketing strategy that is measurable and geared to getting a result. Unlike branding or general marketing strategies, direct response marketing (DRM) is objective. With DRM, I was able to specifically measure my success and have control over what was and wasn't working.

For example, newsletters are a common way to attempt to attract patients into your practice. The problem I have with newsletters is that I'm never sure if they're working or not. How do I track newsletter conversions? It seemed like a one-way conversation that didn't necessarily engage patients or prospects.

I began searching for solutions that were similar to newsletters, because I liked the reach it had with patients, but I wanted to be able to measure results. I discovered an improved method to educate my previous patients while engaging with specific populations. It's called email marketing or direct response marketing via emailing patients. Email marketing allows me to measure important data like how many people are interested in your email (open rates), how many people are interested in your message (click rates), as well as who subscribes to your offer (conversions).

These terms used to be totally foreign to me but today are as familiar as anatomy terms. I realized that in order to keep the practice full of patients, I had to learn marketing lingo and techniques to succeed.

Email marketing is a simple strategy that is 100% controllable by the owner and can be measured and constantly improved.

Can you imagine using a better marketing strategy? I couldn't, and it sure was better than visiting a million doctors.

Here's how I use email marketing:

1. **Write an article or blog post.** Be sure to write about a topic that is of interest to the population you're trying to attract to your clinic.
2. **Create a link to a free piece of information.** For instance, write an article about the five common causes of back pain, then offer a video of three simple home stretches to help back pain. The person has to click on the link to access the PDF or video for the stretches.
3. **Create a compelling subject line.** A subject line is the short description you see on your phone or computer that determines whether you open the email. It's not the

title of the article necessarily, but something that gets the person to do one thing: open the email.

This simple strategy will determine how compelled people were to open your email (i.e., subject line) and how interested in your article and offer they were (i.e., they clicked the link). With this new information, you can target-email the people who watched the video of the free simple back pain exercises.

Utilize the exact same formula as above, but make the offer something more compelling, like a free screen. Again, you will measure the results of your open rates and click rates. However, now you'll measure how many people are converting into "Free Screens." The more screens, the better the chance of turning them into a patient and generating revenue.

This is a very simplified example of how you can use a direct response strategy. DRM is easy to track and quantify. The DRM industry is responsible for generating millions, if not billions of dollars in revenue, both online and offline It flat-out works.

The good news is that it uses Pearson's Law of measuring and tracking results and allows the owner (or a staff member) to be in complete control.

But honestly, the only thing I cared about was results and getting a positive ROI (return on investment). Since the investment is small, the ROI can be huge. The secret is to know how much a new patient is worth to your clinic. If you know this metric, then it's virtually impossible NOT to be successful with this strategy, especially as you get better at discovering what interests your prospects.

As far as technology is concerned, the biggest technical aspect of performing this strategy is using a program to send out the emails. As of now, few EMR software programs have this capability and can track the metrics needed. Two well-known email delivery programs that I have used are **MailChimp** and

Infusionsoft. MailChimp is relatively inexpensive but can send out emails easily while tracking the key metrics. Infusionsoft is a more complex, more expensive program that has many bells and whistles, but for smaller practices it's probably not necessary.

While the first strategy of this chapter focused on getting new leads, this strategy is great for converting leads and/or previous patients into new patients. These two marketing strategies are very powerful and, when used in combination, have completely transformed my practice.

Here are a few tips I learned along the way using these marketing strategies:

Tip #1 – People who know, like, and trust you (i.e., previous patients) are ten times more likely to come back as a new patient.

Tip #2 – People who have already given you money (i.e., previous patients) are ten times more likely to give you money again (i.e., purchase additional services).

Tip #3 – The secret to successful marketing is about testing what works and repeating it. "Don't think—test."

Tip #4 – Delegate these technology-based marketing strategies. DO NOT keep them on your plate.

Strategy Three: Facebook

A great way that we engage with our community and generate new patients is through a company Facebook page. It will take you only a few minutes to set up, but it will give you a forum to educate, engage, and connect with your audience.

Unfortunately, most owners only use their page sporadically, posting every so often. There's no intention or plan behind it, so of course, there are no results. My advice is to use your page not only to let people know what's happening in your practice, but to educate them, similar to the email marketing strategy. Instead of creating new content for your Facebook followers, just use the articles and blogs from the email campaign.

Maybe people will engage more on the Facebook page than with emails. The purpose is to measure your results and offer people a variety of ways to connect with your practice. When you start sending out good information that people like, they begin to take interest in you. Share stories about your staff, whose birthday it is, and new hires. Share interesting things your practice is involved in like upcoming races, talks, and fundraising efforts. Remain mindful of "Likes" and comments. These are engagement measures that help you know what people like. However, Likes aren't enough. They may feel good for a few minutes, but they're not what pays the bills.

Use Facebook to Generate Leads

Once you have a topic or an article that your followers really like, promote it. You can use Facebook to generate leads. Here's how:

1. **Create an Ad on Facebook** – This part is pretty simple, even for non-tech-savvy people (like me). It usually involves a picture and a sentence or two about what they will learn or how to solve a problem.
2. **Determine Your Budget** – You can choose the amount of money you want to spend, the location, the target audiences, etc. The goal is to keep it local to your town and related to other interests your target market may have.

3. **Squeeze Page** – This is a little more involved, but not complicated. A landing page (also known as a squeeze page) is a simple one-page website that houses your offer or freebie. It's an easy way to explain in more detail why someone should either download or purchase your offer. In this case, it's the exercises you're giving away in exchange for a name and email address.

   A squeeze page can also be used to sign up people for seminars, webinars, talks, etc.

> **Tip:** *There are apps and software programs that make it very easy to create squeeze pages. The one I use is called* **Leadpages.**

4. **Create Follow-Up Emails** – This is used to engage further with the person who just gave their email address for the exercise video. Have a couple of emails ready to send out. These can be similar to the emails you've already created for your email campaign.
   a. Email 1 – Thank You email.
   b. Email 2 – Do they have any questions about the exercises? Allow them an easy way to ask questions and engage with you.
   c. Email 3 – Create an offer for a free screen. Use the same strategy as email marketing.

Email process:

Here's a sample response to someone who clicked on a link:

"Hi, John, thank you so much for downloading The Three Simple Exercises for Eliminating Back Pain. Give them a try and let me know if you have any questions."

Two days later you can send another email:

"Hey John, hopefully you had a chance to try out the exercises. By the way, here is another thing you can do that I've done with other patients, that really helped them reduce their back pain. Let me know if it helps."

After one week, send a final email:

"John, I hope the exercises and additional tips helped get rid of your back pain. Just in case you're still having pain, I wanted to offer another option. Many times back pain is caused by muscle spasms that linger or joints that get "stuck" due to sports or overuse activities. If identified and treated quickly, many times you can be 100% pain-free in a matter of days. If you would like for me to take a look, I have a couple of times open, tomorrow at 2 p.m. or Thursday at 5 p.m. Let me know if either of these times work. Looking forward to hearing from you."

All we're doing is capturing the contact information of people who have an interest in your subject matter and allowing them to do something about it. Many times this type of campaign gets overlooked or discounted because it's not very complicated. However, the results speak for themselves, and we have generated many patients using this easy and automated referral process.

The real secret in getting amazing results is how well you follow up. The other benefit is the opportunity to help direct people to get good care. For instance, maybe the person who was interested in your back pain exercises is not from your area. This is a great opportunity for you to deliver value by guiding them to a PT in their area. If you're like me and believe in karma (aka: Law of Attraction) then by helping this person, you will attract good things back to you.

If you don't do it, who will? Where will they get their advice? Google? Web MD? The doctor? Remember, the doctor is going to give patients his own perspective on physical therapy, not ours. Isn't it better that the advice comes from you, the expert on physical therapy, versus someone else?

How to Make This Process Easy

I am NOT in charge of this process. My talent and skill level is with the idea and vision creation. I have been involved in connecting via emails and phone conversations with prospects, as well as performing free screenings. That is a very good use of my time and has generated tens of thousands of dollars in revenue.

However, I have delegated all of the technical aspects of this project. I had PT aides and front desk people help me until I hired a marketing person to do it. Nowadays, you can hire people virtually to create most of this back-end work. Upwork and Fiverr have tons of people who can do practically every aspect of this project.

Once you have the Who, as in who is in charge of this project, I would recommend documenting the entire process. This will allow you to reproduce it anytime you want and to continually make it better. The best part is that once you teach your other clinicians how to communicate with people via email and over the phone, you, the owner, will not have to do it. This will free up your time while your practice gets busier and busier.

For more information specifically on Chapter 11, Digital Age Marketing, please visit:

www.TheAutomatedProfessionalPractice.com/book/chapter11.

CHAPTER 12

The 90-Day Sprint Revisited

In this final chapter, I will dive into how to get your projects moving to accomplish real, tangible results without excess stress.

To be perfectly candid, I struggle with the word "goal." I know it's a part of everything we read and everything we learned in school. However, in the business world I think the word "milestone" is more appropriate and is the word I use with my staff and clients.

A milestone is a success point along a continuous journey. A goal is an ending point of success. I see everything as a continuous journey filled with milestones along the way. However, for the purpose of this chapter, I will use the word goal since this was my thinking as I created my automated practice.

I think you already know that setting goals is good practice and will help you achieve bigger results. Let's face it: We are required to do this for our patients, so of course it's important for our own practices. So why don't most owners do this continuously?

I struggled with this myself for many years. I always had goals of how I wanted things to work out, but they were never written down. I kept them in my head. I always thought that was good enough. Unfortunately, that was the worst place to keep my goals.

No Time for Goal Setting

The biggest reason I didn't write down my goals is because I didn't have time. Of course, I could have set aside the time to do it, but with everything else on my plate I didn't feel that writing down my goals was a top priority. I was already overwhelmed with trying to run a practice, treat my patients, document, and put out fires. Plus, the books I read on goal-setting seemed like a lot of work on my part without adding much benefit.

The other reason I didn't write down goals was because of fear. Now before you ask what fear has to do with goal-setting, allow me to explain. The fear I had was not with hitting my goals; it was the fear of not achieving my goals. In other words, my fragile ego couldn't take "another failure." I was already failing at building my practice, so adding more wood to the fire didn't make sense to me. It was much easier to keep these ideas of growth in my head. I just couldn't handle any more failures on my part.

My Greatest Challenge

The greatest challenge I continued to face in my practice was a lack of vision. Another way to say it was I had no clarity on where I was going and how I was going to get there. I finally realized that goal-setting would help me provide the clarity I and my staff needed to take my practice to the next level, so I hired a consultant.

Her fee was $1,000 and she recommended that I close my office for an entire day. So, I closed my two locations and paid my employees to be a part of this SMART goal process.

By end of the day I had a five-year business growth plan. I had core objectives, committees, and verbal agreements with all 12 of my employees at the time, including part-time people. We had committee chairs with specific goals to achieve. It was beautiful. Back in PT school, I would have received an A+ on this project.

Unfortunately, within six months, 80% of my staff either quit or were let go and the entire plan had collapsed.

I had spent all this time and money on a consultant and in less than six months I was worse off than before. I wasn't sure what to do and didn't know where to turn. Then it hit me. The reason this process didn't work was because the consultant I hired had experience in non-profits and larger companies, not small private practices.

I didn't need a consultant to create a five-year vision for my practice like the big companies. I needed a small business, entrepreneurial way of setting goals and growing a practice. I knew that I needed a real action plan that was focused on my current needs and not on a cookie-cutter process for all companies.

Unfortunately, most of the goal-setting books and systems on the market today are based on old, antiquated models from the industrial age, when technology was in its infancy. However, the world has seemingly changed overnight, and the technology age has leveled the playing field, allowing small companies to accelerate growth. We are living in a fast-paced environment due to an explosion of technology and unlimited knowledge at our fingertips. How can I look five years into the future when the entire future will be completely different in less than two years? I firmly believe a five-year plan is a complete waste of time for small practices because of technology.

At this point, my vision of how to organize my practice became crystal clear. I knew what I had to do, and it didn't require creating complicated and time-consuming five-year plans. In fact, it only required 90 days.

The 90-Day Success Plan

I began looking at my business in 90-day segments. According to some of the well-known entrepreneurs in the business world, 90 days was a perfect amount of time to get a lot accomplished, but wasn't as daunting as looking at two to three years out. I felt I could stay focused for three months. Longer than that was asking a lot, but three months? I could do that.

My idea was to go hard for 90 days, then relax and celebrate. Then repeat the cycle.

The Ideal Day

The first thing I did was create my ideal work day. What would I want a typical day in my practice to look like? I used this as my vision. Instead of some big, mammoth goal that was unrealistic, I just focused on what I wanted a day in the clinic to look like.

- Are you treating patients? How often? How many hours?
- What specifically are you doing in the office during your ideal days?
- Are you in the office every day or sometimes in the office and sometimes outside of the office?
- What is your relationship with your staff?
- Are you working weekends? How many days off do you take?

Feel free to change "ideal day" to "ideal week" if that helps you. I have done both.

As I went through this process, I asked myself, "Where would I be happiest in my practice? What would I be doing? How many days in the clinic would I be treating patients?"

This ultimately led me to consider whether it was possible to not treat, unless I really wanted to, while still maintaining a successful, profitable, small practice.

I wrote down specifically what I'd be doing during my ideal day. The more I envisioned this day, the more excited I got. It became clear to me that my mission was to create this ideal day for my family and me. What I didn't know at the time was how I was going to do it, and what effect it would have on my staff and patients.

The key is to be specific in your targets and imagery. The clearer you can picture your ideal day, the more real it will become in your mind. The less clear it is in your mind, the less likely it is that it will happen.

Reverse Engineering

After you have created your ideal day, the next step is to create your 90-day plan using the process of Reverse Engineering. Once you have your vision of how your practice will run and what role you will have in it (i.e., your ideal day), your next step is to come up with a plan to make it happen.

First, determine what would have to happen in the next 90 days in order to achieve your ideal day or week.

Next, create monthly goals and then weekly goals. Remember the saying: "You eat an elephant one bite at a time." In this case, you're taking your big, audacious vision and breaking it down into:

- 90-Day Segments
- Monthly Goals

- Weekly Goals
- Daily Goals (optional). I stop at weekly goals although some owners break it down further to daily goals.

To summarize, I've taken my vision of my ideal day that's somewhere in the future and have broken it down to manageable 90-day sprints. These 90-day projects now become my focus for the quarter.

Keep Your Plate Clean

By far, the most difficult part in creating my ideal day was actually staying focused long enough to make it happen. One of the biggest mistakes I made in the beginning of starting my practice was placing too many day-to-day activities on my plate.

Several 90-day sprints were focused on removing these non-essential activities from my plate. I knew this would free up my time and move me closer toward my ideal day.

Still, knowing that focus is important and staying focused were two different things. To address this, I began writing down three results I wanted to accomplish each week. These were outside of my normal weekly activities like treating, documentation, and overseeing the staff.

This was the question I asked myself: What result can I accomplish this week that more than any other will lead me to successfully completing my 90-Day sprint?

Although this question sounds simple, it forced me to really reflect and think deeply about what was most important to me to do this week. There are so many areas we could be focusing on and in each area there are several sub-areas that need fixing or updating. However, as I practiced this weekly ritual, my goal-setting and problem-solving skills improved. Soon results followed.

The 8-Step Problem Solver

One of the problem areas I wanted to fix was working weekends. So, I began going through the initial process of asking the question, *"What result can I accomplish this week that, more than any other, will lead me to achieving my 90-Day Sprint?"* I became very clear about what I wanted (to stop working weekends), but I wasn't sure how to get there.

This challenge of not knowing how to solve this problem led me to developing a tool to solve any problem I was facing. This ultimately became The Problem Solver. The Problem Solver is a tool to help you think through problems in a specific way. It is a concept as much as it is a strategy and tactic. Here are the steps involved:

1. **Project Name** – Name your project. It is easier to refer to your project this way instead of having to describe it.
2. **Objective Goal** – Create an objective goal. Use a metric if possible.
3. **Completion Date** – Choose a date within the 90-Day Sprint.
4. **The Meaning** – What will be the results of this project and why are they important to you and/or the practice?
5. **Strategic Brainstorming** – Create options to solve the project objective.
6. **Choose Strategy** – Choose the best option.
7. **Challenges** – Write down all of the barriers, obstacles, and problems you anticipate having while executing this strategy in the form of a question.
8. **Next Smallest Action Step** – The next step to get your project into motion. Weekly goals.

No More Weekends.

Below is an example of how I used the Problem Solver to stop working weekends.

- **Project Name**: No More Weekends
- **Objective**: Stop working weekends completely (currently working Saturdays and some Sundays).
- **Completion Date**: 60 days
- **Meaning**: Reduce my stress level, spend more time with my family, remove undesirable activities from my plate, free up my time, use my time more efficiently.
- **Brainstorming**: Hire a bookkeeper to help with financials, have a current employee handle the financials, find time during the week to do it.
- **Choose Strategy**: Hire a bookkeeper.
- **Challenges**: Can I afford it? How do I choose one? Where do I look?
- **Next Smallest Action Steps**:
  a. Call my Financial Advisor
  b. Search Google
  c. Interview bookkeepers

I hired a bookkeeper in less than two weeks. In fewer than 60 days, I completely stopped working weekends and started to spend more time with my family and doing things I love. This immediately reduced my stress level and helped me move on to solving other problems in my clinic.

Not working weekends was just one project on my way to my ideal week. My ultimate goal was to create a PT practice that didn't require me to be there day-to-day. I used this exact formula, one project at a time and one 90-Day Sprint at a time, to eventually create my ideal day, week, and practice.

The hardest part is getting started and trusting the process.

To this day, I start my week off by deciding on two to three specific results that I want to accomplish. Every 90 days, I create a set of new goals and milestones I want to achieve. The rest of my time is spent executing my plan and solving the problems and challenges that come up along the way.

What's best about this approach to creating your ideal day, week, and practice is that it is doable, realistic, and completely under your control. Of course, it won't be easy because nothing worthwhile is. However, the more you practice these habits, the easier they will become.

> *Results don't take time. It's NOT getting results that takes time.*

The results you will achieve will be unlike anything you have ever experienced. They are a natural reward for permanently solving your problems. Although it took me almost eight years to achieve my Ideal Practice, many other practice owners who are incorporating the principles and concepts found in this book are doing it in a matter of months.

Results don't take time. It's NOT getting results that takes time.

For more information specifically on Chapter 12, The 90-Day Sprint Revisited, please visit:

www.TheAutomatedProfessionalPractice.com/book/chapter12.

Continuing the Conversation

I would like to personally thank you for purchasing my book and taking the first step to building you own automated practice.

At www.TheAutomatedProfessionalPractice.com, we teach practice owners from all disciplines how to remove the constant overwhelming stress of owning a professional practice in the 21st century. We show them how to create financial prosperity well above the norm, and learn how to earn back time by freeing themselves up from the day to day grind of managing a practice.

On my website, you will find dozens of helpful resources from blog posts to videos detailing business strategies that will broaden your perspective and inspire you to take action. All of these resources and more are available for FREE.

For those interested in accelerating this process, I encourage you to learn more about my Practice Building Intensive at www. TheAutomatedProfessionalPractice.com/PBI. This program is for those who are ready for a better quality of life! A life filled with a bigger and brighter future, and a practice that will be the catalyst in helping you achieve it. This multi-day Intensive shows you exactly how to go from where your practice is today to creating a successful and sustaining practice in the next eighteen months.

From one fellow professional practice owner to another, I know the struggles and the roadblocks preventing your success.

Let me help by sharing my 20 plus years of experience as a clinician, manager and leader to help transform your practice and realize your incredible potential. Take back control and stop having others dictate how successful you can be. Your journey does not have to be done alone.

Please visit my website www.TheAutomatedProfessional-Practice.com for more insights and information.

With gratitude,

Jamey

About the Author

Jamey Schrier's PT practice burned down in 2004, which forced him to face the decision to rebuild or walk away. You see, prior to his practice burning down, Jamey was in pain. Not the physical pain many of us treat, but the emotional and mental pain that comes with being the sole owner of a business.

At the time of the fire, Jamey was working 10-12 hours per day, six days a week, doing practically everything in the practice, and barely staying above water. He knew he couldn't keep this up and maintain a balanced home life. He kept asking himself "Is there a better way?"

In 2013, relying more on faith than confidence, Jamey finally did the unthinkable… he took himself completely off the treatment schedule.

However, what happened next surprised everyone, most of all Jamey… that year his business revenue soared to $1.4 million and his profits surpassed the $20,000 per month mark. All of this while not treating a single person the entire year.

In 2014, Jamey created The Automated Practice™ Online Course. The course is a culmination of his business and life experiences over the last 20 years, teaching Clinic Owners exactly how to free themselves from their grueling daily work schedule, how to make more money, and have more free time.

Today, Jamey continues to help entrepreneurial-minded practice owners in the medical, health, and wellness fields automate their practice creating a life full of freedom and opportunity.

Made in the USA
Charleston, SC
20 August 2016